Alphonse Daudet's Short Stories

Little French Masterpieces

LITTLE FRENCH MASTERPIECES

ALPHONSE DAUDET
From a steel engraving

Little French Masterpieces

Edited by

Alexander Jessup

Alphonse Daudet

An Introduction by

William Peterfield Trent

The Translation by

George Burnham Ives

G. P. Putnam's Sons

New York and London

The Knickerbocker Press

1909

ALPHONSE ....
From a steel ....

Little French Masterpieces

Edited by

Alexander Jessup

Alphonse Daudet

An Introduction by

William Peterfield Trent

The Translation by

George Burnham Ives

G. P. Putnam's Sons

New York and London

The Knickerbocker Press

1909

The Knickerbocker Press, New York

Introduction

Alphonse Daudet

(1840–1897)

IT is not necessary to say that the task of
selecting representative stories of Daudet
is rendered difficult chiefly by the remarkable
fecundity, variety, and sustained power of his
genius. But while it is not necessary to say
this, in saying it one really gives the best
reason for undertaking such a task of selec-
tion. For a writer characterised by fecundity,
variety, and sustained power is obviously a
master of his own kind, and it is always pleasant and profitable to endeavour, even if it be
for the thousandth time, to make the work of
a master better known. Now in this busy
age and in this world of many books—even
of many truly good books—it is idle to expect
that the complete work, or a large part of the
work of any master, save perhaps of a few

Introduction

supreme ones, can get itself read by more than a comparatively small section of the reading public. Yet the large, busy public is by no means totally indifferent to the work of the great writers of whom it has heard in a more or less vague way, and it is generally willing to acquaint itself with that work when a convenient opportunity offers. Experience has shown that there is no better way to interest the public in a writer or a group of writers than by presenting it with well-chosen volumes of selections. Think of how many lovers of poetry Palgrave's *Golden Treasury* has made—surely far more than the old editions of *The British Poets* in a hundred or more volumes ever succeeded in making. Just so in the case of Daudet, it seems idle to expect that our own large, alien public can find the time to read, whether in the original or in translation, the whole of his two most important collections of stories and sketches— the *Letters from My Mill* (1869) and the *Monday Tales* (1873). Much less can it be expected to read the prose fantasies collected with his poems, or the tales to be found in *Artists' Wives*, in the volume entitled *La Fédor*, with its descriptive sub-title, *Pages from Life*, or elsewhere among his unfortunately still scattered works.* [See page xxiv.]

For various reasons that need not be detailed, it has seemed best to take the tales and sketches here chosen to represent Daudet from the two volumes named first above. One reason is particularly cogent, to wit, that it was these two collections that Daudet took pains to revise and enlarge, transferring to them stories that appeared first in other collections. For example, the definitive *Letters from My Mill* was augmented by several pieces taken from the *Sketches and Landscapes* that originally followed *Robert Helmont*, but are no longer to be found with that interesting study of war time. So also several stories were transferred from the *Letters to an Absentee* to the *Monday Tales*. Although Daudet, sometimes with good reason, withdrew from circulation not a few of his stories and sketches, it is idle to think that in the case of so great a writer they will remain in oblivion, and it is much to be wished that the work of preparing the needed definitive and inclusive edition of his writings should be begun at once. No thorough study of his evolution as a short-story writer can now be made without the trouble and expense of securing books long out of print.

The two main series of stories (*Letters from My Mill* and *Monday Tales*) contain between sixty and seventy pieces, of which not quite a third have been selected. It is, of course, to be hoped that the new reader of Daudet will be induced to read both collections in full, and that he will pass on to at least two of the inimitably humorous Tartarin books—*Tartarin of Tarascon* and *Tartarin on the Alps*—and to the long series of Daudet's excellent novels—to *Fromont, Jr., and Risler, Sr.*, to *Jack*, to *The Nabob*, to *Kings in Exile*, to *Numa Roumestan*, if to no others. Yet why append the qualify-

Introduction

ing phrase? The reader who has read these books of Daudet is not likely to wish to omit even the books of what is often called his decline—for example, *The Immortal,* with its scathing satire on the French Academy. Nor will such a reader, if he be fairly able to comprehend Continental views on relationships not fully discussed by Englishmen and Americans, care to take leave of Daudet without having read what is probably his strongest and most artistic book—the much discussed *Sapho.* And if he have become a true admirer of Daudet the man — which is what nearly all his readers become — he will be standing greatly in his own light if he do not read that most charming of youthful autobiographies, marred though it be by the romantic, fictitious ending, the inimitable *Little What's His Name.* But this is no place for a catalogue of Daudet's writings.

If, however, the reader of the nineteen stories that follow is not able, for one cause or another, to develop his acquaintance with

Introduction

Daudet into intimacy, he may comfort himself with the thought that he knows the great Frenchman in what is to many of his admirers his most attractive capacity. It is already quite apparent that a number of Daudet's elaborate novels are not wearing well, and it is a question whether more than two or three of them are well enough constructed to bid defiance to time. One may cherish a lively hope that Tartarin in his best estate is destined to live long as a care-dispeller, one may fear that the world will never cease to need the lessons taught by *Sapho,* one may believe that *The Nabob,* with its wonderfully effective scenes and two or three admirably painted portraits, may survive so as by fire. But even Daudet's most devoted readers may well be wary of predicting a very long life for many of his other novels, even for *Numa Roumestan,* with its excellent elements of the true comedy of manners, even for *Fromont, Jr., and Risler, Sr.,* with its distinct power of characterisation, expressed especially in the selfish visionary, Delobelle, the actor out of employment and living on his vanity and his wife and daughter.

It requires much less critical confidence and courage to predict a very long life, if not practical immortality, for Daudet's best short stories. His two chief collections represent in epitome the main elements that critics have discovered in the man and his work. They represent Daudet the poet, with his exquisite fancy, his winning charm, his subtle, indescribable style, his susceptibility to all that is lovely and joyous in nature and in human life; in short, in his sunny, mercurial Provençal temperament. This Daudet is seen in full measure in *Letters from My Mill*, if indeed this book be not the most charming he ever wrote, the one we most often and willingly reread, the one we should choose for a companion if we were limited in our choice. But there was another Daudet more or less superimposed upon this sunny, poetic Daudet, true child of Provence. Upon few Frenchmen of a generation ago did the terrible years of the Franco-Prussian War

Introduction

and the Commune produce a more sobering impression than upon Daudet. The romanticist and poet deepened into a realistic observer of human life in all its phases. Impressions and fancies were more and more supplanted by accurate notes, later carefully worked up into novels that dealt in increasing measure with the tragic, the sordid, the ironical features of life. The poet and humourist did not, of course, disappear; but they struggled with the realist, the satirist, one might almost say, the naturalist. This matured, deepened Daudet, who finds his home and chief interests in seething Paris rather than in peaceful Provence, is seen, not to the full, but to a marked degree and very attractively in the *Monday Tales.* The two stories which a majority of his readers would select as the most pathetic he ever wrote, *The Last Class* and *The Siege of Berlin,* are in this volume. That terrible, almost exaggerated indictment of incompetence in high places, *The Game of Billiards,* is also there, and so is the effective, if somewhat

Introduction

overwrought, *Vision of the Judge of Colmar*, not here translated, but worth reading as an impressive variation on the theme of Dr. Hale's *The Man Without a Country*. *Monday Tales* contains, moreover, some wonderfully vivid sketches of the gruesome sights that met Daudet's eyes during the siege, and thus preludes the realistic work of later years. Yet it has its fantasies and its comedies also. What could be better of its kind than *The Little Pies?* What better than that vivid reminiscence of childish mendacity, *The Pope is Dead*, the forerunner of the posthumous *First Journey, First Falsehood*, itself a curious variation on the theme of Balzac's *A Start in Life?* Still, it can hardly be denied that it is not the lighter things—even such delightful conceptions as that of the Parisian clock that transforms the manners and morals of a respectable Munich family (*The Bougival Clock*)—that give the collection of *Monday Tales* its dominant tone. The book takes its colour for many of us from *The Last Class*, from *The*

Introduction

Siege of Berlin, from pathetic sketches like *Mothers,* from other pictures of the siege, especially from the poignant story here given, *The Child Spy.*

But, important as *Monday Tales* is among Daudet's books and among the world's notable collections of stories, it seems to yield precedence as a book to his earlier collection, *Letters from My Mill.* The old windmill, the writer's local habitation, and the Southern setting, whether of Provence proper or of Corsica or of Algeria, lend the book a unity (more apparent, it is true, than real) and an individuality that *Monday Tales* does not possess. Perhaps its nearest analogue in our own literature is Hawthorne's *Mosses from an Old Manse,* which has a more felicitous title and doubtless appeals to introspective temperaments more than Daudet's expansive masterpiece does. The main point is, however, that both books possess an atmosphere, if we may so phrase it; in the one case a typically Northern, in the other, a typically Southern

Introduction

atmosphere. It is a curious fact that for the Southern analogue to Hawthorne's delightful book, we should have to go to French literature, and not to that other American master of the short story, with his Southern rearing, Edgar Allan Poe. But Poe was at home in a land that has no local colour, and the curious fact just noted becomes all the more curious when we remember what a reception Baudelaire and other Frenchmen have given to Poe's tales. It is pleasant to think of the two republics interchanging books instead of shots, of our lending the French the *Tales of the Grotesque and Arabesque,* of their lending us the *Letters from My Mill.*

As has already been said, the Daudet of the *Letters* is the sunny Provençal poet, the expansive genius who admits us to a charming intimacy. It would be a mistake, however, to suppose that the tales and sketches this poet gives us are mere happy improvisations thrown off in moments of inspiration by an easy, affluent writer full of life and youth.

Introduction

If they were merely this they would still be charming, but one would have good cause to doubt the permanence of their charm. It is because we know from his biographers that Daudet put his best art into these slight stories, that he would spend a day wrestling with an intractable sentence or paragraph, and because we know from the best French critics and feel in our own imperfect way that his style is in every sense individual, flexible, sustained, and exquisite without a trace of weakness, that we are as sure as we can be in such matters that the *Letters from My Mill* will live. We are sure also that such stories as *The Last Class* and *The Siege of Berlin* will live also, but of the permanence of *Monday Tales* as a whole, much more of such a collection as *Artists' Wives,* we may well have a reasonable doubt.

Twelve of our nineteen pieces have been selected from the *Letters* and there are still wonderfully good things left. *The Stars* is an idyll no reader is likely to forget, and

Introduction

immediately upon it follows that pathetic domestic tragedy of the sound-hearted country youth and the depraved town girl (*L'Arlésienne*). The "touch of nature" that makes the whole world kin is found in full measure in *Bixiou's Portfolio;* and much of the sultry, drowsy beauty of the semi-tropics in *At Milianah*. As for the dozen miniature masterpieces here presented, appreciative criticism seems superfluous. Will one soon forget the knife-grinder shrinking from the jeers and taunts of his fellow passengers, or the pathetic secret of the old miller, or that delightfully told apologue of the rash pet of Monsieur Seguin, or the vengeance of the Pope's mule, or the Plutarch of the lighthouse-keeper, or the truly effective sermon of the Abbé Martin, the Jonathan Edwards of Cucugnan, or the appealing picture of the old couple, or the pathetic irony of the death of the little Dauphin? Surely no one can forget these things, and just as surely when stories and sketches stand out as clearly in after months and years as

Introduction

these do, they are to be regarded as master-pieces and as masterpieces of a particularly rare kind. For unless a slight story be extraordinarily well told it slips the mind with surprising facility. But there are still four pieces to mention, none of them inferior, perhaps all of them not merely equal but superior to the tales that have preceded them. *The Legend of the Man with the Golden Brain* is a striking example of the blending of bizarre fancy with deep imagination. *The Three Low Masses* points its moral with a grotesque humour and a picturesque descriptive power, to say nothing of dramatic force, that are rarely found in combination. *The Two Inns* opens up in its eight short pages an almost limitless vista of suffering and patience. Surely Matthew Arnold's phrase "piercing pathos" applies here if it does to anything in literature. Finally, the irony of *The Elixir of the Reverend Father Gaucher,* tempered as it is by Daudet's humour and kindliness, leaves us with a satisfying sense of that fecundity, variety, and sustained power of his genius which was claimed at the beginning of this unnecessary Introduction.

In conclusion, let us make no mistake about our phrase "sustained power." Readers of one of M. Lemaître's delightful appreciations of Daudet will doubtless have carried away the word "charm" as best connoting the character of Daudet's genius and of the effects it produces upon his admirers. Probably no critic has ever written of Daudet without using this indefinable word, or some word or phrase equivalent to it. Daudet's work, whether in his novels or in his stories, lacks the range and the tremendous, overwhelming, titanic impressiveness of Balzac's. For some of us it lacks the firm, the ineluctable art of Maupassant. But it would seem a mistake to suppose that his genius therefore lacks sustained power. There are many kinds of power, and that exerted by charm is not the least potent of them, and perhaps the most continuously satisfying and beneficent. Of

Introduction

this powerful charm, even if it does stop short of enchantment, Daudet, in his brief stories at least, possesses an abundance, and because of this fact his *Letters from My Mill* bids fair to become a possession forever, not merely for France but for the world.

W. P. Trent

* Since the above was written, a complete edition of Daudet's works, in eighteen volumes, has been announced in Paris.

W. P. T.

Letters from My Mill

(1869)

The Beaucaire Diligence

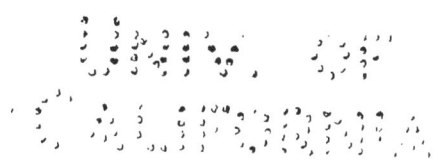

The Beaucaire Diligence

IT was the day of my arrival here. I had
taken the Beaucaire diligence, a respectable old vehicle which had not far to go before
reaching home again, but which sauntered all
along the way, in order to have the appear-
ance at night of arriving from a long distance.
There were five of us on the imperial, without counting the driver.

First, a drover from Camargue, a short,
thick-set, hairy man, with an odour of herds,
and with large bloodshot eyes, and silver
rings in his ears; next, two natives of Beaucaire, a baker and his son-in-law, both very
red-faced and short-breathed, but with magnificent profiles, like two Roman medals with
the image of Vitellius. Lastly, on the box-
seat with the driver, a man—no, a cap, an
enormous rabbit-skin cap, which did not say

[5]

much and gazed at the road with a distressed expression.

All those people knew one another and talked aloud of their affairs very freely. The man from Camargue said that he had come from Nimes, summoned by the examining magistrates because of a blow with a pitch-fork that he had dealt a shepherd. Tempers are quick in Camargue. And what about Beaucaire! Would you believe that our two Beaucairians actually threatened to cut each other's throats on the subject of the Blessed Virgin? It seems that the baker was from a parish devoted from time immemorial to the Madonna, to her whom the Provençals call the Good Mother, and who carries the little Jesus in her arms; the son-in-law, on the contrary, sang in the choir of a brand-new church, consecrated to the Immaculate Conception, that lovely smiling image which is represented with her arms hanging at her sides and her hands full of rays of light. The quarrel arose from that fact. You should

[6]

have seen how those two good Catholics abused each other and their Madonnas :

"A pretty creature your Immaculate One is!"

"Get out with your Good Mother!"

"She saw some fine doings in Palestine, that hussy of yours!"

"And what about yours, hey? The ugly witch! Who knows what she did n't do? Ask St. Joseph."

Nothing save the gleaming of knives was lacking to make us fancy that we were on the wharfs at Naples; and in faith, I believe that that edifying theological contest would have ended in that way if the driver. had not interposed.

"Let us alone with your Madonnas," he said laughingly to the Beaucairians; "that 's all women's nonsense; men ought not to bother with it."

Thereupon he cracked his whip, with a skeptical expression which brought everybody over to his opinion.

[7]

Alphonse Daudet

The discussion came to an end, but the baker, having got started, felt that he must spend the rest of his ammunition, and, turning to the unfortunate cap, which sat silent and melancholy in its corner, he said with a bantering expression:

"And how about your wife, knife-grinder—which parish does she favour?"

Evidently there was some very comical allusion in that question, for the whole imperial roared with laughter. The knife-grinder did not laugh. He did not seem to have heard. Observing that, the baker turned to me:

"You don't know his wife, do you, monsieur? She's a queer kind of a churchwoman! There aren't two like her in Beaucaire."

The laughter redoubled. The knife-grinder did not budge; he simply said in a low tone, without raising his head:

"Hold your tongue, baker."

But that devil of a baker did not propose to hold his tongue, and he continued with greater zest:

The Beaucaire Diligence

"Bless my soul! the fellow is n't to be pitied for having a wife such as she. No man can be bored for an instant with her. Think of it! a beauty who has herself abducted every six months, she always has something to tell you when she comes home. It 's a curious little household, I tell you. Just imagine, monsieur, that they had n't been married a year, when paff! the wife goes off to Spain with a chocolate-peddler. The husband was left alone in his house, to weep and drink. He was like a madman. After some time, the charmer came back to the province dressed as a Spanish woman, with a little tambourine. We all said to her: 'Keep out of his way, or he will kill you.' Kill her! not much! they went to living together again as quietly as you please, and she taught him to play the tambourine."

There was a fresh outburst of laughter. The knife-grinder in his corner muttered again, without raising his head:

"Hold your tongue, baker."

The baker paid no heed, but continued:

"Perhaps you think, monsieur, that after her return from Spain the charmer kept still. Not a bit of it; her husband had taken the thing so well that it made her inclined to try it again. After the Spaniard, it was a military officer, then a boatman on the Rhône, then a musician, then a— I don't know whom. The amusing part of it is that the same comedy is acted every time. The wife goes off, the husband weeps; she returns and he is consoled. And they keep on abducting her, and he keeps on taking her back. Don't you think that the fellow has patience? I must say, however, that the little woman 's mighty pretty—a genuine morsel for a cardinal: dainty, and lively, and well-built; and a white skin, too, and nut-brown eyes that always laugh when she looks at a man. Faith, my Parisian, if you ever pass through Beaucaire——"

"Oh! hold your tongue, baker, I beg you!" said the poor knife-grinder once more, in a heartrending tone.

The Beaucaire Diligence

At that moment the diligence stopped. We were at the farm Des Anglores. The two men from Beaucaire alighted, and I promise you that I did not try to detain them. That wag of a baker! we could hear him laugh after he was in the farmyard.

When they had gone the imperial seemed empty. We had left the man from Camargue at Arles; the driver was walking beside the horses. The knife-grinder and I were alone, each in his corner, saying not a word. It was hot, and the leather of the hood was scorching. At intervals I felt my eyes close and my head become heavy; but it was impossible to sleep. I had always in my ears that "hold your tongue, I beg you," so gentle, yet so heartrending. He did not sleep, either, the poor man; from behind I could see his broad shoulders quivering, and his hand, a long, colourless, stupid hand, tremble on the back of his seat, like the hand of an old man. He was weeping.

"Here you are at home, Parisian," the driver

suddenly called to me; and with the end of his whip he pointed to my green hill with the mill perched upon it like a great butterfly.

I made haste to alight. As I passed the knife-grinder I tried to look under his cap; I was anxious to see his face before leaving him. As if he had understood my thought, the wretched man abruptly raised his head and fastening his eyes upon mine, he said in a hollow voice:

"Look well at me, my friend, and if you hear one of these days that there has been trouble at Beaucaire, you will be able to say that you know the man who did it."

His face was sad and lifeless, with little faded eyes. There were tears in those eyes, but in the voice there was hatred. Hatred is the wrath of the weak! If I were the knife-grinder's wife, I should be on my guard.

Master Cornille's Secret

Master Cornille's Secret

FRANCET MAMAÏ, an old fifer, who comes sometimes to pass the evening with me and drink mulled wine, told me the other evening of a little village drama which my mill witnessed some twenty years ago. The good man's story impressed me, and I propose to try to tell it to you as I heard it.

Imagine for a moment, dear readers, that you are seated before a jar of perfumed wine, and that it is an old fifer who is speaking.

Our province, my dear monsieur, has not always been a dead place, entirely unknown to fame, as it is to-day. Long ago there was a big business done here in grinding grain, and the people from all the farms within a circuit of ten leagues brought us their grain to grind. The hills all around the village were covered with windmills. To right and left one could see nothing but the sails turning about in the mistral above the pines, long strings of little donkeys laden with bags climbing the hills and stretching out along the roads; and it was pleasant to hear all through the week the cracking of the whips on the hilltops, the creaking of the canvas, and the *Dia hue!* of the millers' men. On Sundays we went to the mills in groups. The millers treated to muscat. The millers' wives were as lovely as queens, with their lace neckerchiefs and their gold crosses. I used to carry my fife, and we danced farandoles till it was pitch-dark. Those mills, you see, were the pleasure and wealth of our province.

Unluckily, some Frenchmen from Paris conceived the idea of setting up a steam flour-mill on the road to Tarascon. Very fine and new it was; the people fell into the habit of sending their grain there, and the poor wind-mills were left without work. For some time they tried to keep up the struggle, but steam was the stronger, and one after another, *pécaïre!* they were all obliged to close. We saw no more strings of little donkeys. The millers' pretty wives sold their gold crosses. No more muscat! no more farandoles! No matter how hard the mistral might blow, the sails did not move. Then, one fine day, the commune ordered all those shanties torn down, and vines and olive-trees were planted where they stood.

But, amid all the distraction, one little mill held out and continued to turn bravely on its hill, in despite of the steam-millers. That was Master Cornille's mill, the same one in which we are passing the evening at this moment.

Master Cornille was an old miller, who had lived for sixty years in flour and was crazy over his trade. The setting up of the steam-mills made him act like a madman. For a week he ran about the village, collecting people round him and shouting at the top of his lungs that they intended to poison Provence with the flour from the steam-mills.

"Don't go there," he would say; "those

2

villains use steam to make bread, steam, which is an invention of the devil, while I work with the mistral and the tramontana, which are the breath of the good Lord "; and he would spout a lot of fine words in praise of windmills, but no one listened to them.

Then, in a towering rage, the old man shut himself up in his mill, and lived alone like a wild beast. He would n't even keep with him his granddaughter Vivette, a child of fifteen, who since the death of her parents had no one but her grandfather in the world. The poor child was obliged to earn her living and to hire herself out among the farms for the harvest, the silkworm season, or the olive picking. And yet her grandfather seemed to love the child dearly. He often travelled four leagues on foot in the heat of the sun to see her at the farm where she was working, and when he was with her, he would pass hours at a time gazing at her and weeping.

In the province, people thought that the old miller had been led by avarice to send Vivette away; and it did not do him credit to allow his grandchild to travel about that way from one farm to another, exposed to the brutality of the labourers and to all the trials of young women in service. People thought it very wrong, too, that a man of Master Cornille's reputation, who up to that time had shown the greatest self-respect, should go about through the streets like a regular gypsy, bare-footed, with a cap all holes and a blouse all in rags. The fact is that on Sunday, when we saw him come in to mass, ⁴we were ashámed for him, we old men; and Cornille felt it so keenly that he did n't dare to come and sit in the warden's pew; he always remained at the back of the church, near the holy-water vessel, with the poor.

There was something in Master Cornille's life we could n't understand. For a long time no one in the village had carried him any grain, and yet the sails of his windmill were always in motion as before. In the evening, people met the old miller on the roads driving before him his donkey loaded with fat bags of flour.

"Good evening, Master Cornille," the peasants would call out to him; "is business still good?"

"Still good, my children," the old man would reply, with a jovial air. "Thank God, we have no lack of work."

Then, if any one asked where in the devil so much work could come from, he would put a finger to his lips and answer gravely:

"Hush! I am working for exportation."

No one could ever get anything more from him.

As for putting one's nose inside his mill, it was n't to be thought of. Even little Vivette herself never went in there.

When people passed in front of it, they always found the door closed, the huge sails moving, the old ass browsing on the platform, and a great thin cat taking a sun-bath on the window-sill, and glaring at them with a wicked expression.

All this smelt of mystery, and made people talk a great deal. Every one had his own explanation of Master Cornille's secret, but the general report was that there were even more bags of silver in the mill than bags of grain.

After a while, however, everything came to light; this is how it happened:

One fine day, as I was playing on my fife for the young people to dance, I noticed that my eldest boy and little Vivette had fallen in love with each other. At heart I was not displeased, because after all the name of Cornille was held in honour among us; and then it would have pleased me to see that pretty little bird of a Vivette trotting about my house. But as our lovers had often had opportunities to be together, I determined, for fear of accidents, to settle the business at once, and I went up to the mill to say a word to the grandfather. Ah! the old sorcerer! you should have seen how he received me! It was impossible for me to induce him to open his

[21]

door. I explained my reasons after a fashion, through the keyhole; and all the time I was talking, there was that lean villain of a cat snorting like a devil over my head.

The old man did n't give me time to finish, but shouted to me most impolitely to go back to my fife; that if I was in such a hurry to marry my boy, I could go and look for a girl at the steam-mill. As you can imagine, the blood went to my head when I heard such rough talk; but I was wise enough to restrain myself, and leaving the old fool in his mill, I returned to inform the children of my discom-fiture. The poor lambs could n't believe it; they asked me as a favour to allow them to go up together to the mill and speak to the grand-father. I had n't the courage to refuse, and off my lovers went.

Just as they reached the mill, Master Cornille had gone out. The door was securely locked; but the old fellow, when he went away, had left his ladder outside, and suddenly it occurred to the children to go in by the window and see what there might be inside that famous mill.

What a strange thing! the main room of the mill was empty. Not a sack, not a particle of grain; not the slightest trace of flour on the walls or on the spider-webs. They could n't even smell that pleasant, warm odour of ground wheat that makes the air of a mill so fragrant. The shaft was covered with dust and the huge thin cat was sleeping on it.

The lower room had the same aspect of poverty and neglect: a wretched bed, a few rags, a crust of bread on one stair, and in a corner three or four bursted sacks, with rubbish and plaster sticking out.

That was Master Cornille's secret! it was that plaster that he paraded at night on the roads, to save the honour of the mill and to make people think that he made flour there. Poor mill! poor Cornille! Long ago the steam-millers had robbed them of their last customer. The sails still turned, but the mill ground nothing.

Alphonse Daudet

The children returned to me all in tears and told me what they had seen. It tore my heart to listen to them. Without a moment's loss of time I ran to the neighbours; I told them the story in two words, and we agreed instantly that we must carry to Cornille's mill all the wheat there was in the houses. No sooner said than done. The whole village started off, and we arrived at the top of the hill with a procession of donkeys loaded with grain, and real grain, too!

The mill was wide-open. In front of the door Master Cornille sat on a bag of plaster, weeping, with his face in his hands. He had discovered on returning home that during his absence some one had entered his mill and discovered his sad secret.

"Poor me!" he said. "Now there's nothing left for me to do but to die. The mill is dishonoured."

And he sobbed as if his heart would break, calling his mill by all sorts of names, speaking to it as if it was a living person.

Master Cornille's Secret

At that moment the donkeys arrived on the platform and we all began to shout as we did in the palmy days of the millers:

"Holla! mill there! holla! Master Cornille!"

And the bags were piled up before the door and the fine red grain strewed the earth in all directions.

Master Cornille stared with all his eyes. He took up some grain in the hollow of his old hand, and said, laughing and weeping at once:

"It is grain! Lord God! real grain! Leave me; let me look at it."

Then, turning to us:

"Ah! I knew that you'd come back to me. All those steam-millers are thieves."

We proposed to carry him in triumph to the village.

"No, no, my children," he said; "first of all I must give my mill something to eat. Just think! it's so long since he has had anything between his teeth!"

And it brought the tears to the eyes of us all to see the poor old man rush about to right and left, emptying the sacks, looking after the millstone, while the grain was crushed and the fine wheaten dust rose to the ceiling.

I must do our people justice: from that day we never allowed the old miller to lack work. Then one morning Master Cornille died, and the sails of our last mill ceased to turn—this time forever. When Cornille was dead, no one followed in his footsteps. What can you expect, monsieur? Everything has an end in this world, and we must believe that the day of windmills has passed, like that of barges on the Rhône, parliaments, and jackets with big flowers.

The Goat of Monsieur Seguin

The Goat of Monsieur Seguin

To M. Pierre Gringoire, Lyrical Poet at Paris

YOU will always be the same, my poor Gringoire!

Think of it! you are offered the place of reporter on a respectable Paris newspaper, and you have the assurance to refuse! Why, look at yourself, unhappy youth! look at that worn-out doublet, those dilapidated breeches, that gaunt face, which cries aloud that it is hungry. And this is where your passion for rhyme has brought you! this is the result of your ten years of loyal service among the pages of my lord Apollo! Are n't you ashamed, finally?

Be a reporter, you idiot; be a reporter! You will earn honest crowns, you will have your special seat at Brébant's, and you will be able to appear every first night with a new feather in your cap.

No? You will not? You propose to remain perfectly free to the end? Well! just listen to the story of Monsieur Seguin's goat. You will see what one gains by attempting to remain free.

Monsieur Seguin had never had good luck with his goats. He lost them all in the same way; some fine morning they broke their cord and went off to the mountain, and there the wolf ate them. Neither their master's petting, nor fear of the wolf, nor anything else deterred them. They were, it would seem, independent goats, determined to have fresh air and liberty at any price.

Honest Monsieur Seguin, who was unable to understand the temperament of his beasts, was dismayed. He said:

"I am done; the goats are bored at my house, and I won't keep another one."

However, he did not get discouraged, and

The Goat of Monsieur Seguin

after losing six goats all in the same way, he bought a seventh; but that time he was very careful to buy a very young one, so that it would be more likely to become accustomed to living with him.

Ah! Monsieur Seguin's little kid was such a pretty thing, Gringoire! with her soft eyes, her little beard like a subaltern's, her gleaming black hoofs, her striped horns, and her long white hair, which formed a sort of greatcoat! She was almost as lovely as Esmeralda's goat — do you remember, Gringoire? And then, so docile, too, and affectionate, allowing herself to be milked without moving, without putting her foot into the pail. A perfect little love of a kid!

Monsieur Seguin had an enclosure behind his house, surrounded by hawthorn. There he placed his new boarder. He fastened her to a stake, in the place where the grass was the richest, taking care to give her a long rope; and from time to time he went to see if she was all right. The kid was very happy and browsed with such zest that Monsieur Seguin was overjoyed.

"At last," thought the poor man, "I have one that will not be bored here!"

Monsieur Seguin was mistaken; his kid was bored.

One day she said to herself, looking up at the mountain:

"How happy they must be up there! what pleasure to gambol about in the heather, without this infernal cord that galls one's neck! It is all right for the donkey or the ox to graze in an enclosed place, but goats need plenty of room."

From that moment, the grass in the enclosure seemed distasteful. Ennui assailed the kid. She grew thin, her milk became scanty. It was painful to see her pulling at her cord all day long, with her head turned towards the mountain, her nostrils dilated, and bleating sadly.

Monsieur Seguin noticed that something was the matter with the kid, but he did not know what it was. One morning as he finished milking her, the kid turned her head and said to him in her dialect:

"Listen, Monsieur Seguin; I am dying in your enclosure; let me go to the mountain."

"Ah! *mon Dieu!* this one, too!" cried Monsieur Seguin in stupefaction; and the shock caused him to drop his pail; then, seating himself on the grass beside his kid, he said:

"What, Blanquette, do you want to leave me?"

And Blanquette replied:

"Yes, Monsieur Seguin."

"Have n't you enough grass here?"

"Oh, yes! Monsieur Seguin."

"Perhaps you are tied too short; do you want me to lengthen the rope?"

"It is n't worth while, Monsieur Seguin."

"What is it that you want, then?"

"I want to go to the mountain, Monsieur Seguin."

"Why, you wretched creature, don't you

3   [83]

know that there is a wolf in the mountain?
What will you do when he comes?"

"I will butt him with my horns, Monsieur
Seguin."

"The wolf does n't care for your horns. He
has eaten goats with horns much longer than
yours. Don't you remember poor Renaude
who was here last year? A fine goat, as
strong and ill-tempered as any he-goat. She
fought with the wolf all night, and then in the
morning the wolf ate her."

"*Pécaïre!* poor Renaude! but that does n't
make any difference to me, Monsieur Seguin;
let me go to the mountain."

"Divine mercy!" exclaimed Monsieur Seguin; "what on earth does somebody do to
my goats? Still another one that the wolf
will end by eating! But no! I will save you
in spite of yourself, you hussy! and as I am
afraid that you will break your rope, I am
going to shut you up in the stable, and you
shall always stay there."

Thereupon Monsieur Seguin carried the kid

to a dark stable, the door of which he locked securely. Unluckily he forgot the window, and he no sooner had his back turned than the little creature took her leave.

Do you laugh, Gringoire? Parbleu! of course you do; you are of the faction of the goats, against poor Monsieur Seguin. We will see if you laugh in a moment.

When the white kid arrived in the mountain there was general rejoicing. Never had any of the old fir-trees seen anything so pretty. They welcomed her like a little queen. The chestnuts bent to the ground to caress her with their branches. The golden heather opened for her to pass, and gave forth the sweetest perfume that it could. The whole mountain celebrated her arrival.

You can imagine, Gringoire, whether our kid was happy! No more ropes, no more stakes, nothing to prevent her from gamboling and grazing at her pleasure. That was the place where the grass grew! above the tips of her horns, my dear fellow! And such grass! fine and sweet, made up of a thousand different plants. It was a very different thing from the grass in the enclosure. And the flowers — great blue bellflowers, purple fox-gloves with long stamens, a whole forest of wild flowers, overflowing with intoxicating juices.

The white kid, half tipsy, played about there with her legs in the air, and rolled down the slopes, with the falling leaves and the chestnuts; then, of a sudden, she sprang to her feet with one leap. Away she went, with her head thrust forward, through the under-brush and the thickets, sometimes on a peak, sometimes in the bottom of a ravine, up and down and everywhere. You would have said that there were ten of Monsieur Seguin's kids in the mountain.

The fact is that Blanquette was afraid of nothing. She crossed with one bound broad torrents which spattered her, as she passed, with misty spray and foam. Then, dripping wet, she stretched herself out on a flat rock and allowed the sun to dry her. Once, as she crept to the edge of a plateau with some clover in her teeth, she spied below her, in the plain, Monsieur Seguin's house with the enclosure behind it. That made her laugh until she cried.

"How tiny it is!" she said; "how was I ever able to live there?"

Poor dear! finding herself perched up there so high, she believed herself to be at least as large as the world.

In fact that was a great day for Monsieur Seguin's kid. About midday, as she ran to right and left, she happened upon a band of chamois which were busily engaged in eating wild grapes. Our little white-robed vagrant created a sensation. They gave her the best place at the vine, and those gentlemen were all very gallant. Indeed it seems — this between ourselves, Gringoire — that a young chamois with a black coat had the good fortune to please Blanquette. The two lovers lost themselves in the woods for an hour or two, and if you would know what they said to each other, go ask the chattering streams that flow invisibly under the moss.

Suddenly the wind freshened. The mountain turned purple; it was evening.

"Already!" said the little kid; and she stopped, much surprised.

The fields below were drowned in mist. Monsieur Seguin's enclosure disappeared in the haze, and of the cottage she could see only the roof, with a thread of smoke. She listened to the bells of a flock being driven home, and her heart was heavy. A falcon, flying homeward, brushed her with his wings as he passed. She started. Then there arose a howl in the mountain:

"Hou! hou!"

She thought of the wolf; during the day the wild creature had not given him a thought. At the same moment a horn blew in the valley. It was good Monsieur Seguin making a last effort.

"Hou! hou!" howled the wolf.

The Goat of Monsieur Seguin

"Come back! come back!" cried the horn.

Blanquette longed to go back; but when she remembered the stake, the rope, and the hedge about the enclosure, she thought that she could never again become accustomed to that life, and that it was better to stay where she was.

The horn ceased to blow.

The kid heard a rustling of leaves behind her. She turned and saw in the darkness two short, straight ears and two gleaming eyes. It was the wolf.

He sat there on his haunches, enormous, motionless, gazing at the little white kid and licking his chops in anticipation. As he felt sure that he should eat her, the wolf was in no hurry; but when she turned, he began to laugh wickedly.

"Ha! ha!" Monsieur Seguin's little kid!" and he passed his great red tongue over his lean chops.

Blanquette felt that she was lost. For a

moment, as she remembered the story of old Renaude, who had fought all night only to be eaten in the morning, she thought that it would be better to be eaten then; then, thinking better of it, she stood on guard, her head down and her horns forward, like the brave Seguin goat that she was. Not that she had any hope of killing the wolf,— kids do not kill wolves — but simply to see if she could hold out as long as Renaude.

Thereupon the monster came forward and the little horns began to play.

Ah! the dear little kid, how courageously she went at it! More than ten times — I am not lying, Gringoire — she compelled the wolf to retreat in order to take breath. During these momentary respites, the little glutton hastily plucked another blade of her dear grass; then she returned to the battle with her mouth full. This lasted all night. From time to time Monsieur Seguin's kid glanced at the stars dancing in the clear sky and said to herself:

The Goat of Monsieur Seguin

"Oh! if only I can hold out until dawn!"

One after another the stars went out. Blanquette fought with redoubled fury with her horns, the wolf with his teeth. A pale gleam appeared on the horizon. The hoarse crowing of a cock came up from a farm.

"At last!" said the poor creature, who was only awaiting the dawn to die; and she lay down in her lovely white coat all spotted with blood.

Thereupon the wolf threw himself upon the little kid and ate her.

Adieu, Gringoire!

The story you have heard is not a fable of my invention. If ever you come to Provence our farmers will often speak to you of "the goat of Monsieur Seguin, that fought the wolf all night, and then, in the morning, the wolf ate her up."

You understand, Gringoire :

"And then, in the morning, the wolf ate her up."

The Pope's Mule

The Pope's Mule

OF all the clever sayings, proverbs, or saws
with which our Provence peasants em-
bellish their discourse, I know of none more
picturesque or more peculiar than this. Within
a radius of fifteen leagues of my mill, when
anybody mentions a spiteful, vindictive man,
he will say: "Look out for that man! he is
like the Pope's mule, that keeps her kick for
seven years."

I tried for a long time to find out the source
of that proverb, what that Papal mule might
be, and that kick kept for seven years. No
one here was able to give me any information
on that subject, not even Francet Mamaï, my
fife-player, who, however, has the whole leg-
endary history of Provence at his finger-ends.
Francet agrees with me that there is probably
some old tradition of Provence behind it; but

he has never heard it mentioned except in the proverb.

"You won't find that anywhere except in the Grasshoppers' Library," said the old fifer, with a laugh.

I thought the suggestion a good one, and as the Grasshoppers' Library is right at my door, I shut myself up there for a week.

It is a wonderful library, splendidly stocked, open to poets day and night, the attendants being little librarians with cymbals, who play for you all the time. I passed some delight-ful days there, and after a week of investiga-tion—on my back—I ended by discovering what I wanted to know, that is to say, the story of my mule and of that famous kick stored up for seven years. The tale is a pretty one, although slightly ingenuous, and I am go-ing to try to tell it to you as I read it yester-day morning in a manuscript of the colour of the weather, which had a pleasant smell of dry lavender, with long gossamer-threads for book-marks.

The Pope's Mule

He who never saw Avignon in the time of the Popes has seen nothing. Never was there such a city for gayety, life, animation, and a succession of fêtes. There were, from morning till night, processions, pilgrimages, streets strewn with flowers and carpeted with magnificent tapestries, cardinals arriving by the Rhône, with banners flying; gayly bedecked galleys, the soldiers of the Pope singing in Latin on the squares, and the bowls of mendicant friars; and then, from roof to cellar of the houses that crowded humming about the great Papal palace, like bees about their hive, there was the tick-tack of the lace-makers' looms, the rapid movement of the shuttles weaving gold thread for the vestments, the little hammers of the carvers of burettes, the keyboards being tuned at the lute-makers', the songs of the sempstresses; and, overhead, the clang of the bells, and always a tambourine or two jingling down by the bridge. For with us, when the common people are pleased, they must dance and dance; and as the streets in the city in those days were too narrow for the farandole, the fifes and the tambourines stationed themselves on Avignon Bridge, in the cool breezes from the Rhône; and there the people danced and danced, day and night. Ah! the happy days! the happy city! Halberds that did not wound, state prisons where they put wine to cool. No famine; no wars. That is how the Popes of the Comtat governed the people; that is why the people regretted them so bitterly.

There was one especially, a good old fellow, whom they called Boniface. Ah! how many tears were shed in Avignon when he died! He was such a good-natured, affable prince! He laughed so heartily from the back of his mule! And when you passed him—though you were simply a poor little digger of madder, or the provost of the city—he would give you his blessing so courteously! He was a genuine Pope of Yvetot, but of a Provençal Yvetot, with a something shrewd in his laughter, a sprig of marjoram in his biretta, and never a sign of a Jeanneton. The only Jeanneton that the old man had ever been known to have was his vineyard, a tiny vineyard which he had planted himself, three leagues from Avignon, among the myrtles of Château Neuf.

Every Sunday, after vespers, the excellent man went to pay court to it; and when he was there, seated in the warm sun, with his mule by his side and his cardinals lying at the foot of the stumps all about, then he would order a bottle of native wine opened,— that fine, ruby-coloured wine which was called afterwards the Château Neuf of the Popes,— and he would drink it in little sips, looking at his vineyard with a tender expression. Then, when the bottle was empty and the day drew to a close, he would return merrily to the city, followed by all his chapter; and when he rode over Avignon Bridge, through the drums and farandoles, his mule, stirred by the music, would fall into a little skipping amble, while he himself marked the time of the dance with his cap, which scandalised his cardinals terribly, but caused the people to say: "Ah! the kind prince! ah! the dear old Pope!"

Next to his vineyard at Château Neuf, the thing that the Pope loved best on earth was his mule. The good man fairly doted on the beast. Every night, before going to bed, he would go to see if his stable was securely fastened, if anything was lacking in the crib; and he never rose from the table until a huge bowl of wine *à la Française,* with plenty of sugar and spices, had been prepared under his own eye, which he carried to the mule himself, despite the comments of his cardinals. It should be said, too, that the beast was worth the trouble. It was a fine black mule, dappled with red, sure-footed, with a glossy coat, a broad, full rump; and she carried proudly her slender little head, all bedecked with plumes, and ribbons, and silver bells and streamers; and as gentle as an angel withal, with a mild eye and two long ears always in motion, which gave her a most amiable aspect. All Avignon respected her, and when she passed through the streets there was no attention which the people did not pay her; for they all knew that that was the best way to be in favour at court, and that, with her innocent look, the Pope's mule had led more than one to wealth; witness Tistet Védène and his wonderful adventures.

This Tistet Védène was in truth an impudent rascal, whom his father, Guy Védène, the gold-carver, had been obliged to turn out of his house, because he refused to do any work and led the apprentices astray. For six months he was seen dragging his jacket through all the gutters of Avignon, but principally in the neighbourhood of the Papal palace; for the rogue had had for a long while a scheme of his own about the Pope's mule, and you will see what a mischievous scheme it was.

One day, when his Holiness all alone was

riding by the ramparts on his steed, behold my Tistet approaches him, and says, clasping his hands with an air of admiration:

"Ah! *mon Dieu!* what a fine mule you have, Holy Father! Just let me look at her. Ah! what a lovely mule, my Pope! the Emperor of Germany has not her like."

And he patted her and spoke softly to her, as to a maiden:

"Come, my jewel, my treasure, my pearl."

And the excellent Pope, deeply moved, said to himself:

"What a nice little fellow! How nice he is with my mule!"

And what do you suppose happened the next day? Tistet Védène exchanged his old yellow jacket for a fine lace alb, a violet silk hood, and shoes with buckles; and he entered the household of the Pope, to which only sons of nobles and nephews of cardinals had ever been admitted. That is what intrigue leads to! But Tistet Védène did not stop there.

The Pope's Mule

Once in the Pope's service, the rascal continued the game that had succeeded so well.
Insolent with everybody else, he reserved his
attention and care for the mule alone; and
he was always to be seen in the courtyard of
the palace, with a handful of oats or a bunch
of clover, whose purple clusters he shook as
he glanced at the Holy Father's balcony, as if
he would say: "Look! for whom is this?"
The result was that the excellent Pope finally,
feeling that he was growing old, left it to him
to look after the stable and to carry the mule
her bowl of wine *à la Française;* which did
not make the cardinals laugh.

Nor the mule either — it did not make her
laugh. Now, when the time for her wine
arrived, she always saw five or six little clerks
of the household enter her stable and hastily
bury themselves in the straw with their
hoods and their lace; then, after a moment,
a delicious odour of caramel and spices
filled the stable, and Tistet Védène appeared,

carefully carrying the bowl of wine *à la Française.* Then the poor beast's martyrdom began.

That perfumed wine which she loved so dearly, which kept her warm, which gave her wings, they had the fiendish cruelty to bring to her manger, to let her inhale it, and then, when her nostrils were full of it, off it went! the beautiful rose-coloured liquor disappeared down the throats of those young rogues. And if they had only contented themselves with stealing her wine! but all those little clerks were like devils when they had been drinking. One pulled her ears, another her tail; Quiquet mounted her back, Béluguet tried his cap on her head, and not one of the scamps reflected that with a sudden kick the excellent beast could have sent them all into the polar star, or even farther. But no! not for nothing is one the Pope's mule, the mule of benedictions and indulgences. Let the boys do what they would, she did not lose her temper, and she bore a grudge to

Tistet Védène alone.   But he—when she felt
him behind her, her hoofs fairly itched, and in
good sooth there was reason for it.   That
ne'er-do-well of a Tistet played her such
cruel tricks!   He conceived such fiendish ideas
after drinking!

—Would you believe that one day he took it
into his head to make her go up with him
into the belfry, way up to the highest point
of the palace!   And this that I am telling you
is not a fable — two hundred thousand Provençals saw it.   Just imagine the terror of that
wretched beast, when, after twisting blindly
about for an hour on a winding staircase,
and climbing I know not how many stairs,
she suddenly found herself on a platform
dazzling with light; and a thousand feet below
her, a whole fantastic Avignon, the stalls in
the market no larger than walnuts, the Pope's
soldiers in front of their barracks like red
ants, and yonder, over a silver thread, a little
microscopic bridge where the people danced
and danced.   Ah! the poor creature! what a

panic! All the windows in the palace shook with the bray that she uttered.

"What's the matter? What are they doing to her?" cried the good Pope, rushing out upon the balcony.

"Ah! Holy Father, this is what's the matter! Your mule — *mon Dieu!* what will become of us! — your mule has gone up into the belfry."

"All alone?"

"Yes, Holy Father, all alone. See! look up there. Don't you see the ends of her ears hanging over, like two swallows!"

"Merciful Heaven!" exclaimed the poor Pope, raising his eyes. "Why, she must have gone mad! Why, she will kill herself! Will you come down here, you wretched creature?"

Pécaïre! She would have asked nothing better than to have come down; but how? As to the staircase, that was not to be thought of; it is possible to go up such things; but in going down there is a chance to break one's legs a hundred times. And the poor mule was in despair; as she wandered about the platform with her great eyes filled with vertigo, she thought of Tistet Védène.

"Ah! You villain, if I escape, what a kick to-morrow morning!"

That idea of a kick restored a little of her courage; save for that, she could not have held out. At last they succeeded in taking her down; but it was a difficult task. They had to lower her in a litter, with ropes and a jack-screw. And you can imagine what a humiliation it was for the Pope's mule to be suspended at that height, swinging about with her hoofs in the air, like a butterfly at the end of a string. And all Avignon looking at her!

The wretched beast did not sleep that night. It seemed to her all the time that she was walking about on that infernal platform, with the city laughing below her; then she thought of that infamous Tistet Védène, and of the dainty kick that she proposed to give him in the morning. Ah! my friends, what a kick! they would see the smoke at Pampérigouste.

Now, while this pleasant reception was in store for him at the stable, what do you suppose Tistet Védène was doing? He was going down the Rhône, singing, on one of the Pope's galleys, on his way to the Court of Naples, with a party of young nobles whom the city sent every year to Queen Joanna, for training in diplomacy and in refined manners. Tistet was not of noble birth; but the Pope desired to reward him for the care he had bestowed upon his mule, and above all for the activity he had displayed during the day of rescue.

Imagine the mule's disappointment the next morning!

"Ah! the villain! he suspected something!" she thought, as she shook her bells savagely; "but never mind, you scoundrel! you shall have it when you come back, that kick of yours; I will keep it for you!"

And she did keep it for him.

After Tistet's departure, the mule resumed

her quiet mode of life and her former habits.
No more Quiquet or Béluguet in her stable.
The blissful days of wine *à la Française* had
returned, and with them good humour, the
long siestas, and the little dancing step when
she crossed Avignon Bridge. Since her mis-
fortune, however, she was always treated
rather coldly in the city. People whispered
together as she passed; the old folks shook
their heads, and the children laughed as they
pointed to the belfry. Even the worthy Pope
himself had not his former confidence in his
friend, and when he allowed himself to take a
little nap on her back, on Sundays, when he
returned from his vineyard, he always had
this thought: "Suppose I should wake up on
the platform up there!"

The mule saw that and she was unhappy
over it, although she said nothing; but when
the name of Tistet Védène was mentioned
in her presence, her long ears quivered, and
with a short laugh she would sharpen the iron
of her little shoes on the pavement.

Seven years passed thus; and then, at the end of those seven years, Tistet Védène returned from the Court of Naples. His time there was not at an end; but he had learned that the Pope's chief mustard-bearer had died suddenly at Avignon, and as the office seemed to him a good one, he returned in great haste to apply for it.

When that schemer of a Védène entered the great hall of the palace, the Holy Father had difficulty in recognising him, he had grown so tall and so stout. It should be said also that the Pope had grown old too, and that he could not see well without spectacles.

Tistet was not frightened.

"What? don't you recognise me, Holy Father? It is Tistet Védène."

"Védène?"

"Why yes, you know, the one who used to carry the French wine to your mule."

"Oh, yes! I remember. A good little fellow, that Tistet Védène! And what does he want of us now?"

The Pope's Mule

"Oh! a mere nothing, Holy Father. I came to ask you — by the way — have you still your mule? And is she well? Good! — I came to ask you for the place of the chief mustard-bearer, who has just died."

." You, chief mustard-bearer! why, you are too young. How old are you?"

"Twenty years and two months, illustrious pontiff; just five years older than your mule. Ah! blessed palm of God! the excellent beast! If you only knew how I loved that mule! how I sighed for her in Italy! — Won't you let me see her?"

"Yes, my child, you shall see her," said the kind-hearted Pope, deeply touched. "And as you are so fond of the excellent beast, I propose that you shall live near her. From this day, I attach you to my person as chief mustard-bearer. My cardinals will make an outcry, but so much the worse! I am used to it. Come to us to-morrow, when vespers is done, and we will deliver the symbols of your office, in the presence of our chapter, and then — I will take you to see the mule, and you shall come to the vineyard with us both. Ha! ha!—Now go!"

If Tistet Védène was pleased when he left the great hall, I need not tell you how impatiently he awaited the ceremony of the morrow. Meanwhile, there was some one in the palace still happier than he and even more impatient; that was the mule. From the hour of Védène's return until vespers of the following day, the bloodthirsty creature did not cease stuffing herself with oats, and kicking at the wall with her hind feet. She, too, was preparing for the ceremony.

On the morrow, then, when vespers was at an end, Tistet Védène entered the courtyard of the Papal palace. All the high clergy were there, the cardinals in their red robes, the advocate of the devil in black velvet, the convent abbés with their little mitres, the churchwardens of the Saint-Agrico, the violet hoods of the household, the lower clergy too, the Pope's soldiers in full uniform, the three brotherhoods of penitents, the hermits from Mount Ventoux with their fierce eyes, and the little clerk who walks behind them carrying the bell, the Flagellants naked to the waist, the red-faced sacristans in gowns like judges — all, yes, all, even to those who hand the holy-water, and he who lights and he who extinguishes the candles; not one was missing. Ah! it was a grand installation! Bells, fireworks, sunlight, music, and, as always, those mad tambourine-players leading the dance yonder on Avignon Bridge.

When Védène appeared in the midst of the assemblage, his presence and his handsome face aroused a murmur of admiration. He was a magnificent Provençal, of the blond type, with long hair curled at the ends and a small, unruly beard which resembled the shavings of fine metal from the graving-tool of his father the goldsmith. The report was current that the fingers of Queen Joanna had sometimes toyed with that light beard; and Sire de Védène had in truth the vainglorious air and the distraught expression of men whom queens have loved. That day, to do honour to his nation, he had replaced his Neapolitan clothes by a jacket with a pink border *à la Provençale*, and in his hood floated a long plume of the Camargue ibis.

Immediately upon his entrance, the chief mustard-bearer bowed with a noble air, and walked toward the high dais, where the Pope awaited him, to·deliver·the symbols of his office: the spoon of yellow wood and the saffron-coloured coat. The mule was at the foot of the staircase, all saddled and ready to start for the vineyard. When he passed her, Tistet Védène smiled affably and stopped to pat her two or three times in a friendly way on the back, looking out of the corner of his eye to see if the Pope noticed him. The position was excellent. The mule let fly:

"There! take that, you villain! For seven years I have been keeping it for you!"

And she gave him a terrible kick, so terrible that the smoke of it was seen from far Pampérigouste, an eddying cloud of blond smoke in which fluttered an ibis-feather — all that remained of the ill-fated Tistet Védène!

A mule's kick is not ordinarily so disastrous; but she was a Papal mule; and then, think of it! she had kept it for him for seven years. There is no finer example of an ecclesiastical grudge.

The Lighthouse of the Sanguinaires

The Lighthouse of the Sanguinaires

L AST night I was unable to sleep. The mistral was in angry mood, and the outbursts of its loud voice kept me awake until morning. The whole mill creaked, heavily swaying its mutilated sails, which whistled in the wind like the rigging of a ship. Tiles flew from its dilapidated roof. In the distance the pines with which the hill is covered waved to and fro and rustled in the darkness. One might have fancied oneself at sea.

It reminded me perfectly of my notable insomnia three years ago, when I was living at the lighthouse on the Sanguinaires — on the Corsican coast at the mouth of the Bay of Ajaccio.

Another charming little corner that, which I had found, to dream, and to be alone.

Alphonse Daudet

Imagine an island of a reddish colour and of uncivilised aspect; the lighthouse at one end, at the other an old Genoese tower, where an eagle lived in my day. Below, at the water's edge, a ruined lazaretto, overgrown everywhere by weeds; and then, ravines, *maquis,* high cliffs, a few wild goats, and small Corsican horses gamboling about with flying manes; and lastly, high in the air, amid a whirlwind of sea-birds, the lighthouse with its platform of white masonry, where the keepers walked to and fro, the green door with its arched top, the little cast-iron tower, and above, the huge lantern flashing in the sunlight and giving light even during the day. Such was the island of the Sanguinaires as I saw it again last night while I listened to the roaring of my pines. It was to that enchanted isle that I used sometimes to retire, when I longed for fresh air and solitude, before I owned a mill.

What did I do there? What I do here, or even less. When the mistral or the tramon-

tana did not blow too hard, I would seat myself between two rocks at the water's edge,
amid the gulls, and blackbirds, and swallows,
and I would stay there almost all day in
that sort of stupor and delicious prostration
which are born of gazing at the sea. You
know, do you not, that pleasant intoxication
of the mind? You do not think; nor do you
dream. Your whole being escapes you, flies
away — is scattered about. You are the gull
that plunges into the sea, the spray that floats
in the sunlight between two waves — the
white smoke of yonder steamer rapidly dis-
appearing, that little coral boat with the red
sail, that drop of water, that fleck of mist —
anything except yourself. Oh! how many
hours of half-slumber and of mental disper-
sion have I passed on my island!

On the days when the wind was high, the
shore no longer being tenable, I would shut
myself up in the courtyard of the lazaretto,
a small, melancholy courtyard, fragrant with
rosemary and wild absinthium; and there,

sheltered behind a fragment of the old wall, I would allow myself to be gently overcome by the vague perfume of neglect and sadness which floated about with the sunlight in the stone cells, open on all sides like ancient tombs. From time to time, the closing of a gate, a light leap in the grass—it was a goat coming to browse, out of the wind. On seeing me, she would stop in alarm, and stand there before me, sharp-eyed, with her horns in the air, looking down on me with a childlike expression.

About five o'clock, the speaking-trumpet of the keepers summoned me to dinner. Then I would take a narrow path through the *maquis,* rising almost perpendicularly from the sea, and I would return slowly to the lighthouse, turning at every step to gaze at the boundless horizon of water and of light, which seemed to expand as I went higher.

Above it was delightful. I can still see that pleasant dining-room with its floor of broad flags, with its oaken wainscoting, the *bouil-labaisse* smoking in the centre, the door wide-open on the white terrace, and the setting sun streaming in. The keepers were always there, awaiting my arrival to sit down to din-ner. There were three of them, a Marseillais and two Corsicans, all short and bearded, with the same tanned and wrinkled faces and the same goatskin caps; but entirely different in manner and in mood.

The ways of life of these men betrayed at once the difference between the two races. The Marseillais, active and industrious, always full of business, always in motion, ran about the island from morning till night, gardening, fishing, collecting gull's-eggs, lying in wait in the *maquis* to milk a goat on the wing; and always some *aioli* or stew in process of manufacture.

The Corsicans, on the other hand, did abso-lutely nothing outside their duties as keepers; they looked upon themselves as functionaries, and passed the whole of every day in the kitchen, playing endless games of *scopa*, pausing only to light their pipes with a solemn air, and to cut with scissors, in the hollow of their hand, the huge leaves of green tobacco.

For the rest, Marseillais and Corsicans alike were honest, simple, artless fellows, full of attentions for their guest, although after all he must have seemed to them a most extraordinary personage.

Think of it! the idea of shutting oneself up in a lighthouse for pleasure! And they found the days so long, and were so happy when it was their turn to go ashore. In the summer, that great happiness happened once a month. Ten days ashore for every thirty days at the light, that is the rule; but in winter there is stormy weather, and the rules do not hold. The wind blows, the sea rises, the Sanguinaires are white with foam, and the keepers on duty are blockaded two or three months in succession, and sometimes under terrible circumstances.

Lighthouse of the Sanguinaires

"This is what happened to me, monsieur," said old Bartoli one day while we were eating dinner,—"this is what happened to me five years ago, at this very table that we are sitting at, one winter's night, as it is now. That night, there was only two of us in the light, a man named Tchéco and myself. The others were ashore, sick or on leave, I forget which now. We were finishing our dinner as quietly as possible. All of a sudden my comrade stops eating, looks at me a minute with a funny expression, and pouf! down he falls on the table with his arms out. I go to him, and shake him, and call him:

"'I say, Tché! O Tché!'

"Not a word! He was dead. You can imagine my state. I sat there more than an hour, dazed and trembling beside that corpse, and then all of a sudden the thought came to me: 'And the light!' I had just time to go up into the lantern and light it. It was dark already. Such a night, monsieur! the sea and the wind did n't have their natural voices.

Alphonse Daudet

Every minute it seemed to me as if somebody was calling to me on the stairs. And
with it all, such a fever and such a thirst!
But you could n't have induced me to go
down; I was too much afraid of death. However, at daybreak my courage came back a
little. I put my comrade on his bed, with
a sheet over him, then I said a bit of a prayer
and set the alarm signal. Unluckily the sea
was too high; it did n't make any difference
how much I signalled, nobody came. And
there I was alone in the lighthouse with my
poor Tché, and God only knows how long.
I hoped I could keep him with me till the
boat came; but after three days, it was n't
possible. What was I to do? Carry him
outside? Bury him? The rock was too
hard, and there 's so many crows on the
island. It was a pity to abandon that good
Tchéco to them. Then it occurred to me to
take him down to one of the cells in the
lazaretto. That sad task took me a whole
afternoon, and I tell you it took courage.

Lighthouse of the Sanguinaires

Look you, monsieur, even to-day, when I go down to that part of the island on a windy afternoon, it seems to me as if I had the dead man still on my shoulders."

Poor old Bartoli; the sweat rolled down his cheeks, just from thinking of it.

Our meals passed in this way, with plenty of conversation: the lighthouse, the sea, stories of shipwreck and of Corsican bandits. Then, at nightfall, the keeper who had the first watch lighted his little lamp, took his pipe, his drinking-cup, a huge volume of Plutarch with red edges — the whole library of the Sanguinaires — and disappeared. A moment later, there was throughout the house a rattling of chains and pulleys and great clock weights being wound up.

During that time, I sat outside on the terrace. The sun, already very low, sank more and more quickly towards the water, dragging the whole horizon after it. The wind freshened, the island turned purple.

[77]

·Alphonse Daudet

In the sky, close to me, a great bird· flew heavily by: it· was the eagle from the Genoese tower returning home. · Little by little the mist rose.from the sea. Soon one could see only the white rim of foam around the island. Suddenly, over my head, a great flood of soft light gushed forth. The lantern was lighted. Leaving the whole island in shadow, the clear light fell upon the sea, and I sat there lost in darkness, beneath those great luminous rays which barely splashed me as they passed. But the wind grew fresher and fresher. I had no choice but to go inside. I closed the great door by feeling, and secured the iron bars; then, still feeling my way, I ascended a little iron staircase which rang and trembled under my feet, and arrived at the top of the lighthouse. There, there was light enough, on my word.

Imagine·a gigantic Carcel lamp,~ with six rows of wicks, around which the walls of the lantern move slowly, some filled with an enormous crystal lens, the others opening·on a great stationary sash, which shelters the flame from the wind. On entering I was dazzled. Those brasses and pewters, those tin reflectors, the convex crystal walls turning with great bluish circles, all that quivering and clashing of lights made me dizzy for a moment.

Gradually, however, my eyes became accustomed to it, and I would take my seat at the foot of the lamp, beside the keeper, who was reading his Plutarch aloud, for fear of falling asleep.

Outside, darkness and the abyss. On the small balcony which surrounds the lantern the wind rushes howling like a madman. The lantern creaks, the sea roars. On the point of the island, over the reefs, the waves break like cannon-shot. At times an invisible finger raps on the glass: some night-bird, attracted by the light, dashing his head against the lens. In the warm, glowing lantern, nothing save the spitting of the flame, the dropping of the oil, the noise of the chain as it

unwinds, and a monotonous voice intoning
the life of Demetrius.

At midnight the keeper rose, casting a last
glance at his wicks, and we went down. On
the stairs we met the comrade of the second
watch coming up, rubbing his eyes; the cup
and the Plutarch were passed to him. Then,
before going to bed, we entered for a moment
the room at the back, all littered with chains,
with great weights, with pewter reservoirs,
and with ropes; and there, by the light of his
little lamp, the keeper wrote on the lighthouse
log, that lay always open:

"Midnight. Heavy sea. Storm. Sail in
the offing."

The Curé of Cucugnan

The Curé of Cucugnan

EVERY year, at Candlemas, the Provençal poets publish at Avignon a merry little book filled to the covers with fine verses and pretty tales. Last year's has just reached me, and I find in it a delicious fabliau, which I am going to try to translate for you, shortening it a little. Hold out your sacks, Parisians. It is the very cream of Provençal flour that I am going to serve you this time.

Abbé Martin was Curé of Cucugnan.

As good as bread, as honest as gold, he loved his flock like a father; in his eyes his Cucugnan would have been paradise on earth, if the people had given him a little more satisfaction. But alas! the spiders spun their webs in his confessional, and on glorious Easter day the consecrated wafers lay untouched in the holy pyx. The good priest's heart was torn, and he constantly prayed to God that he might not die before he had brought back his scattered flock to the fold.

Now you are about to see that God heard him.

One Sunday, after the Gospel, Monsieur Martin ascended the pulpit.

"Brethren," he said, "you may believe me or not, as you please; the other night I, miserable sinner that I am, found myself at the gate of paradise.

"I knocked; St. Peter opened the gate.

"'Ah! is it you, my dear Monsieur Martin,' he said; 'what good wind blows you here? And what can I do for you?'

"Blessed St. Peter, who keep the record and the keys, could you tell me, if I am not too inquisitive, how many of the people of Cucugnan you have here in paradise?'

"'I cannot refuse you anything, Monsieur Martin; sit down and we will look over the book together.'

The Curé of Cucugnan

"And St. Peter took down his big book, opened it, and put on his spectacles.

"'Now let us see: Cucugnan, you say. Cu-Cu-Cucugnan, here we are. Cucugnan. My worthy Monsieur Martin, the page is entirely blank. Not a soul; no more Cucug-nanese than there are fish-bones in a turkey.'

"'What! nobody from Cucugnan here? Nobody? It is impossible! Pray look again.'

"'No one, holy man. Look for yourself, if you think that I am jesting.'

"I stamped the ground, —pécaire!—and, with clasped hands, I prayed for mercy. Thereupon St. Peter said:

"'Look you, Monsieur Martin, you mustn't turn your heart upside down like this, for you might burst a blood-vessel. It isn't your fault, after all. Your Cucugnanese, you see, must be doing their little quarantine in purgatory for sure.'

"'Oh! in the name of charity, great St. Peter, let me at least see them, and console them!'

Alphonse Daudet

"'Willingly, my friend. Here, put on these sandals at once, for the roads are not very good. That's all right; now, walk straight ahead. Do you see the bend in the road yonder? You will find there a silver gate all studded with black crosses, at the right. Knock, and it will be opened. *Adessias!* keep well and hearty!'

"And I walked on and on. What a journey! My hair stands on end even to think of it. A narrow path, full of thorns, of shiny insects, and of hissing serpents, led me to the silver gate.

"Tap! tap!

"'Who knocks?' asked a hoarse, mournful voice.

"'The Curé of Cucugnan.'

"'Of what?'

"'Of Cucugnan.'

"'Ah! Come in.'

"I went in. A tall, handsome angel, with wings as black as night and a robe as brilliant as day, with a diamond key hanging at his girdle, was writing — cra,—cra — in a book larger than that of St. Peter.

" 'Well, what do you want, and whom have you come to see ?' asked the angel.

" 'Beautiful angel of God, I wish to know —I am very inquisitive, perhaps—if you have the Cucugnanese here ?'

" 'The who ?'

" 'The Cucugnanese, the people from Cucugnan; I am their pastor.'

" 'Ah! Abbé Martin, is it not ?'

" 'At your service, Monsieur angel.'

" 'Cucugnan, you say——'

"And the angel opened his great book and turned the leaves, moistening his finger with saliva, so that the leaves would slip better.

" 'Cucugnan,' he said with a deep sigh; 'Monsieur Martin, we have no one from Cucugnan in purgatory.'

" 'Jesus! Mary! Joseph! no one from Cucugnan in purgatory! Great God! where are they, then ?'

" 'Why, holy man, they are in paradise.

Where in the deuce do you suppose they are ?'

"'But I have just come from paradise.'

"'You have just come from there! well ?'

"'Well! they are not there. Ah! Blessed Mother of the angels!'

"'What do you suppose, monsieur le curé? If they are neither in paradise nor in purgatory, as there is no half-way place, they must be ——'

"'Blessed crucifix! Jesus, Son of David! *Ai! ai!* is it possible? Can it be that great St. Peter lied? Still, I did not hear the cock crow! *Ai!* poor I! how can I go to paradise if my Cucugnanese are not there ?'

"'Look you, my poor Monsieur Martin, as you wish to be sure of all this, let it cost what it may, and to see the truth with your own eyes, take this path, and run if you know how to run. You will find on the left a great gateway. There you will learn everything. God grant it!'

And the angel closed the gate.

[88]

The Curé of Cucugnan

"It was a long path, all paved with red-hot embers. I staggered as if I had been drinking; at every step I stumbled; I was drenched; every hair on my body had its drop of sweat and I was panting with thirst. But thanks to the sandals which kind St. Peter had lent me, I did not burn my feet.

"When I had made enough missteps clumping along, I saw at my left a gate — no, a gateway, an enormous gateway, open wide, like the door of a huge oven. Oh! such a spectacle, my children! There nobody asked me my name; and there was no register. You enter there in crowds, and without obstacle, my brethren, as you enter the wine-shops on Sunday.

"The sweat poured from me in great drops, and yet I was stiff with cold; I shuddered. My hair stood on end. I smelt burning, roasting flesh, something like the smell which spreads through Cucugnan when Eloy the horseshoer burns the hoofs of an old ass, to shoe her. I lost my breath in that putrid, scorching air; I heard a horrible outcry: groans and howls and oaths.

"'Well! are you coming in, or are n't you?' asked a horned demon, pricking me with his fork.

"'I? I am not coming in. I am a friend of God.'

"'You are a friend of God? Well then, you scabby beast, what are you doing here?'

"'I have come—ah! don't mention it, for I can hardly stand on my legs—I have come—I have come a long way, to ask you humbly, if—if, by any chance—you happen to have here any one—any one from—from Cucugnan?'

"'Ah! God's fire! you play the fool, as if you did n't know that all Cucugnan is here. See, you ugly crow, look about you, and you will see how we deal with your precious flock here.'

"And I saw in the midst of a frightful whirl-wind of flame:

"Tall Coq-Galine—you all know him,

brethren — Coq-Galine, who used to get drunk so often, and shook his fleas on his poor Clairon.

"I saw Catarinet, that little hussy, with her nose in the air, who slept all alone in the barn. You remember her, my rascals! But let us go on; I have said too much of her.

"I saw Pascal Doigt-de-Poix, who made his oil with Monsieur Julien's olives.

"I saw Babet the gleaner, who, when she gleaned, in order to make up her bundle more quickly, took handfuls from the sheaves.

"I saw Master Grapasi, who oiled the wheel of his barrow so carefully.

"And Dauphine, who sold the water from his well so dear.

"And Le Tortillard, who, when he met me carrying the Sacrament, went his way, with his cap on his head and his pipe in his mouth, as proud as Artaban, as if he had met a dog.

"And Coulau with his Zette, and Jacques, and Pierre, and Toni ——"

Intensely moved, white with fear, the congregation groaned, as they saw, through the open jaws of hell, this one his father, this one his mother, this one his grandmother, and this one his sister.

" 'You must see, brethren,' continued worthy Abbé Martin, 'you must realise that this cannot last. I have charge of your souls, and I am determined to save you from the abyss into which you are in a fair way to plunge head foremost. To-morrow I shall go to work —no later than to-morrow. And work will not be lacking. This is how I shall go about it. In order that all may go well, we must do everything in an orderly manner. We will work row by row, as they do at Jonquières when they dance.

" To-morrow, Monday, I will confess the old men and the old women. That is nothing.

" Tuesday, the children. That will not take long.

" Wednesday, the boys and girls. That may take some time.

The Curé of Cucugnan

"Thursday, the men. We will cut that short.

"Friday, the women. I will say: 'No lies!'

"Saturday, the miller! One day will not be too much for him alone.

"And if we have finished Sunday, we shall be very lucky.

"You see, my children, when the grain is ripe, we must cut it; when the wine is drawn, we must drink it. We have plenty of soiled linen — it is our business to wash it and to wash it thoroughly.

"That is the grace that I wish you. Amen!"

What was said was done. The washing was done.

Since that memorable Sunday, the perfume of the virtues of Cucugnan can be smelt ten leagues away.

And the worthy pastor, Monsieur Martin, happy and light-hearted, dreamed the other night that, followed by his whole flock, he climbed in a gorgeous procession, amid lighted candles, a cloud of fragrant incense, and choir-boys singing the Te Deum, the brilliantly lighted road to the City of God.

And this is the story of the Curé of Cucug-nan, as I was ordered to tell it you by that tall rascal of a Roumanille, who heard it himself from some other jovial fellow.

Old Folks

Old Folks

" A letter, Father Azan ?"
" Yes, monsieur, it comes from Paris."

He was as proud as a peacock that it came from Paris, was excellent Father Azan. But not I. Something told me that that Parisian epistle from Rue Jean-Jacques, falling upon my table unexpectedly and so early in the morning, would make me lose my whole day. I was not mistaken; see for yourself:

" You must do me a favour, my friend. You must close your mill for one day and go at once to Eyguières—Eyguières is a large village three or four leagues from you, just a pleasant walk. On arriving there, you will ask for the orphan convent. The next house to the convent is a low house with gray shutters, and a small garden behind. You will go in without knocking—the door is always open—and as you enter, you will say

7   [97]

Alphonse Daudet

in a very loud voice: "Good day, my good people! I am Maurice's friend!' Then you will see two old folks—oh! very old, immeasurably old — who will hold out their arms to you from the depths of their great easy-chairs, and you will embrace them for me, with all your heart, as if they were your own people. Then you will talk; they will talk about me; nothing but me; they will tell you a thousand foolish things, which you will listen to without laughing.—You won't laugh, will you?— They are my grandparents, two people whose whole life I am, and who have not seen me for ten years. Ten years is a long while! but what can you expect? Paris holds me tight, and their great age holds them. They are so old, that if they should come to see me they would fall to pieces on the way. Luckily, you are in the neighbourhood, my dear miller, and, while embracing you, the poor people will think that they are embracing me to some extent. I have so often written to them of you and of the warm friendship——"

Old Folks

The devil take our friendship! It happened to be magnificent weather that morning, but not at all appropriate for walking on the road; too much mistral and too little sunshine — a genuine Provençal day. When that infernal letter arrived, I had already chosen my *cagnard* (place of shelter) between two rocks, and I was dreaming of staying there all day, like a lizard, drinking light, and listening to the song of the pines. However, what was I to do? I closed the mill, grumbling, and put the key under the door. My stick and my pipe, and I was off.

I reached Eyguières about two o'clock. The village was deserted; every soul was in the fields. Under the elms of the farmyards, white with dust, the grasshoppers were singing as in the heart of Crau. There was an ass taking the air on the square, in front of the mayor's office, and a flock of pigeons on the church fountain; but no one to point out to me the way to the orphanage. Luckily an old fairy appeared of a sudden, sitting in her

[99]

doorway and spinning. I told her what I was looking for; and as that fairy was very powerful, she had only to raise her distaff: instantly the orphan convent rose before me as if by magic. It was a high, gloomy, dark building, proud to be able to show, above its ogive doorway, an old cross of red sandstone with some Latin words around it. Beside it, I saw another smaller house. Gray shutters and a garden behind. I recognised it instantly, and I entered without knocking.

As long as I live I shall never forget that long, quiet, cool corridor, with its pink walls, the little garden quivering at the rear through a curtain of light colour, and over all the panels faded flowers and lyres. It seemed to me as if I were entering the house of some old bailiff of the days of Sedaine. Through a half-opened door at the end of the corridor, on the left, I could hear the ticking of a big clock, and the voice of a child, but of a child of school age, reading and pausing after each word: " Then — St. — I-re-næ-us — cried —

I—am—the—grain—of—the—Lord.—I—must
—be—ground—by—the—teeth—of—these—
an-i-mals."

I approached the door softly and looked
in.

In the peaceful half-light of a small bedroom, a good old man with red cheeks,
wrinkled to the ends of his fingers, was
sleeping in an easy-chair, with his mouth
open and his hands on his knees. At his
feet a little girl dressed in blue — big cape and
little cap, the costume of the convent — was
reading the life of St. Irenæus from a book
larger than herself. That miraculous reading
had produced its effect upon the whole household. The old man was sleeping in his chair,
the flies on the ceiling, the canaries in their
cage at the window. The great clock snored,
tick-tack, tick-tack. There was nothing awake
in the whole chamber save a broad band
of light which entered, straight and white,
through the closed shutters, full of living
sparks and microscopic waltzes. Amid the

general drowsiness, the child gravely continued her reading: "In-stant-ly— two —lions—rushed —up—on — him—and — ate— him—up." It was at that moment that I entered. The lions of St. Irenæus rushing into the room would not have produced greater stupefaction than I did. A genuine stage effect! The little girl shrieked, the great book fell, the flies and canaries woke, the clock struck, the old man sat up with a start, greatly alarmed, and I myself, slightly disturbed, halted in the doorway and shouted very loud:

"Good day, good people! I am Maurice's friend."

Oh, if you had seen the poor old man then; if you had seen him come towards me with outstretched arms, embrace me, shake my hands, and run wildly about the room, exclaiming:

"*Mon Dieu! mon Dieu!*"

Every wrinkle in his face laughed. His cheeks flushed, and he stammered:

Old Folks

"Ah! monsieur; ah! monsieur."

Then he hurried towards the end of the room, calling:

"Mamette! Mamette!"

A door opened, there was a mouselike tread in the hall; it was Mamette. Nothing could be prettier than that little old woman, with her shell-shaped bonnet, her nun's gown, and the embroidered handkerchief which she held in her hand, to do me honour, after the ancient fashion. It was a most touching thing — they actually resembled each other. With a tower of hair and yellow shells, he too might have been named Mamette. But the real Mamette must have wept bitterly during her life, and she was even more wrinkled than the other. Like the other, too, she had with her a child from the orphanage, a little nurse in a blue cape, who never left her; and to see those two people cared for by those two orphans was the most touching picture that one could imagine.

When she came in, Mamette began by

making me a low reverence, but the old man cut it in two by a word:

"This is Maurice's friend."

Instantly she began to tremble and weep, she lost her handkerchief, turned red, red as a peony, even redder than he. Those old people had but a single drop of blood in their veins, and at the slightest emotion it rushed to their faces.

"Quick, quick, a chair!" said the old woman to her little one.

"Open the shutters," cried the old man to his.

And, each taking me by a hand, they trotted to the window, which was thrown wide open that they might the better see me. The easy-chairs were brought, and I stationed myself between them on a folding-chair, the little blue girls behind us, and the questioning began.

"How is he? What is he doing? Why doesn't he come to see us? Is he happy?" and *patati!* and *patata!* that sort of thing for hours.

For my part, I answered all their questions to the best of my ability, giving such details concerning my friend as I knew, and unblushingly inventing those that I did not know; above all, being careful not to confess that I had never noticed whether his window closed tightly, or what colour the paper was on the walls of his bedroom.

"The paper of his bedroom! it is blue, madame, a light blue, with flowers."

"Really?" said the poor old woman, deeply moved; and she added, turning towards her husband: "He is such a good boy!"

"Oh, yes; he is a good boy!" said the other, enthusiastically.

And all the time I was talking, they exchanged little nods of the head, little sly laughs, and winks, and significant glances; or else the old man would stoop over and say to me:

"Speak louder. She's a little hard of hearing."

And she, on her side:

"A little louder, please! he does n't hear very well."

Thereupon I would raise my voice; and both would thank me with a smile; and in those faded smiles, leaning towards me, seeking in the depths of my eyes the image of their Maurice, I, for my part, was deeply moved to find that image in theirs — vague, veiled, almost intangible, as if I saw my friend smiling at me, a long way off, in a mist.

Suddenly the old man sat erect in his chair.

"Why, it just occurs to me, Mamette—perhaps he has not breakfasted!"

And Mamette, in dismay, tossed her arms into the air:

"Not breakfasted! Great Heaven!"

I thought that they were still talking about Maurice, and I was about to reply that that excellent youth never waited later than noon for his breakfast. But no, they were talking about me; and you should have seen the commotion when I confessed that I was still fasting.

Old Folks

"Lay the table quick, my little blues; the table in the middle of the room, and the Sunday cloth, the flowered plates. And let's no' laugh so much, if you please; and make haste."

I should say that they did make haste. They had hardly had time to break three plates when the breakfast was ready.

"A nice little breakfast," said Mamette, as she led me to the table, "but you will be all alone. We have already eaten this morning."

Poor old people! at no matter what time you take them, they have always eaten that morning.

Mamette's nice little breakfast consisted of two fingers of milk, some dates, and a *barquette,* something like a shortcake; enough to support her and her canaries for at least a week. And to think that I alone consumed all those provisions! What indignation about the little table! How the little blues whispered as they nudged each other; and yonder in their cage, how the canaries seemed to say to each other: "Oh! see that gentleman eating the whole *barquette !*"

I did eat it all, in truth, and almost without noticing it, occupied as I was in looking about that light, peaceful room, where the air was filled with an odour as of ancient things. Above all, there were two little beds from which I could not remove my eyes. Those beds, almost cradles, I imagined as they looked in the morning at daybreak, when they were still hidden behind their great French curtains. The clock strikes three. That is the hour when all old people wake.

"Are you asleep, Mamette?"

"No, my dear."

"Is n't Maurice a nice boy?"

"Oh! he is a nice boy, indeed."

And I imagined a long conversation like that, simply from having seen those two little beds standing side by side.

Meanwhile, there was a terrible drama taking place at the other end of the room, before the cupboard. It was a matter of reaching on the top shelf a certain jar of brandied cherries, which had been awaiting Maurice ten years, and which they desired to open in my honour.

Despite the entreaties of Mamette, the old man had insisted upon going to get the cherries himself; and, having mounted a chair, to his wife's great alarm, he was trying to reach them. You can imagine the picture—the old man trembling and standing on tiptoe, the little blues clinging to his chair, Mamette behind him, gasping, with outstretched arms, and over all a faint perfume of bergamot, which exhaled from the open cupboard and .from the great piles of unbleached linen. It was delightful.

At last, after many efforts, they succeeded in taking the famous jar from the cupboard, and with it an old silver cup, all marred and dented, Maurice's cup when he was small. They filled it for me with cherries to the brim; Maurice was, so fond of cherries! and while serving me the old man whispered in my ear with the air of an epicurean:

"You are very lucky, you are, to have a chance to eat them. My wife made them herself. You are going to taste something good."

Alas! his wife had made them, but she had forgotten to sweeten them. What can you expect? People become absent-minded as they grow old. Your cherries were atrocious, my poor Mamette. But that did not prevent me from eating them to the last one, without a wink.

The repast at an end, I rose to take leave of my hosts. They would have been glad to keep me a little longer, to talk about the good boy; but the day was drawing to a close, the mill was far away, and I must go.

The old man rose as I did.

"My coat, Mamette. I am going with him to the square."

Surely Mamette believed in her heart that it was already a little cool for him to escort me to the square, but she made no sign. However, while she was helping him to put his arms into the sleeves of his coat, a fine coat of the colour of Spanish snuff, I heard the dear creature whisper to him:

"You won't stay out too late, will you?"

And he, with a little sly look:

"Ha! ha! I don't know—perhaps."

At that they looked at each other with a laugh, and the little blues laughed to see them laugh, and the canaries in their corner laughed also in their way. Between ourselves, I believe that the odour of the cherries had intoxicated them all a little.

The night was falling when the grandfather and I went out. The little blue followed us at a distance, to take him home; but he did not see her and he was as proud as possible to walk on my arm, like a man. Mamette, with radiant face, saw that from her doorstep, and as she watched us, she nodded her head prettily, as if to say:

"Never mind, he can still walk, my poor old man!"

The Death of the Dauphin

The Death of the Dauphin

THE little Dauphin is sick; the little Dauphin is going to die. In all the churches of the realm the Blessed Sacrament is exposed night and day, and tall candles are burning for the recovery of the royal child. The streets in the old residence are sad and silent, the bells no longer ring, the carriages go at a footpace. About the palace the curious citizens watch through the iron grills the porters with gilt paunches talking in the courtyards with an air of importance.

The whole château is in commotion. Chamberlains, majordomos, run hastily up and down the marble staircases. The galleries are full of pages and of courtiers in silk garments, who go from group to group asking news in undertones. On the broad steps weeping maids of honour greet one another with low courtesies, wiping their eyes with pretty embroidered handkerchiefs.

In the orangery there is a great assemblage of long-robed doctors. Through the windows they can be seen flourishing their long black sleeves and bending majestically their hammer-like wigs. The little Dauphin's governor and equerry walk back and forth before the door, awaiting the decision of the faculty. Scullions pass them by without saluting them. The equerry swears like a heathen, the governor recites lines from Horace. And meanwhile, in the direction of the stables one hears a long, plaintive neigh. It is the little Dauphin's horse, calling sadly from his empty manger.

And the king? Where is monseigneur the king? The king is all alone in a room at the end of the château. Majesties do not like to be seen weeping. As for the queen, that is a different matter. Seated at the little Dauphin's pillow, her lovely face is bathed in tears, and she sobs aloud before them all, as a linen-draper's wife might do.

The Death of the Dauphin

In his lace-bedecked crib the little Dauphin, whiter than the cushions upon which he lies, is resting now with closed eyes. They think that he sleeps; but no. The little Dauphin is not asleep. He turns to his mother, and seeing that she is weeping, he says to her:

"Madame queen, why do you weep? Is it because you really believe that I am going to die?"

The queen tries to reply. Sobs prevent her from speaking.

"Pray do not weep, madame queen; you forget that I am the Dauphin, and that dauphins cannot die like this."

The queen sobs more bitterly than ever, and the little Dauphin begins to be alarmed.

"I say," he says, "I don't want Death to come and take me, and I will find a way to prevent his coming here. Let them send at once forty very strong troopers to stand guard around our bed! Let a hundred big guns watch night and day, with matches lighted,

under our windows! And woe to Death if
it dares approach us!"

To please the royal child the queen makes
a sign. In a moment they hear the big guns
rumbling through the courtyard; and forty
tall troopers, halberds in hand, take their places
about the room. They are all old soldiers
with gray mustaches. The little Dauphin
claps his hands when he sees them. He re-
cognises one of them and calls him:

"Lorrain! Lorrain!"

The soldier steps forward towards the bed.
"I love you dearly, my old Lorrain. Let
me see your big sword. If Death tries to take
me you must kill him, won't you?"

"Yes, monseigneur," Lorrain replies. And
two great tears roll down his bronzed cheeks.

At that moment the chaplain approaches
the little Dauphin and talks with him for a
long time in a low voice, showing him a
crucifix. The little Dauphin listens with an
expression of great surprise, then, abruptly
interrupting him, he says:

The Death of the Dauphin

"I understand what you say, monsieur l'abbé; but tell me, could n't my little friend Beppo die in my place, if I gave him a lot of money?"

The chaplain continues to speak in a low voice, and the little Dauphin's expression becomes more and more astonished.

When the chaplain has finished, the little Dauphin replies with a deep sigh:

"All this that you tell me is very sad, monsieur l'abbé; but one thing consoles me, and that is that up yonder, in the paradise of the stars, I shall still be the Dauphin. I know that the good Lord is my cousin, and that He cannot fail to treat me according to my rank."

Then he adds, turning to his mother:

"Let them bring me my richest clothes, my doublet of white ermine and my velvet slippers! I wish to make myself handsome for the angels, and to enter paradise in the costume of a Dauphin."

A third time, the chaplain leans towards the little Dauphin and talks to him for a long time in a low voice. In the midst of his harangue, the royal child angrily interrupts:

"Why then, to be Dauphin is to be nothing at all!"

And, refusing to listen to anything more, the little Dauphin turns towards the wall and weeps bitterly.

The Legend of the Man with the
Golden Brain

The Legend of the Man with the Golden Brain

ON reading your letter, madame, I had a feeling of remorse. I was angry with myself for the rather too doleful colour of my stories, and I am determined to offer you to-day something joyous, yes, wildly joyous.

For why should I be melancholy, after all? I live a thousand leagues from Parisian fogs, on a hill bathed in light, in the land of tambourines and muscat wine. About me, everything is sunshine and music; I have orchestras of finches, choruses of tomtits; in the morning the curlews say: "Cureli! cureli!"; at noon, the grasshoppers; and then the shepherds playing their fifes, and the lovely dark-faced girls whom I hear laughing among the vines. In truth, the spot is ill-chosen to paint in black; I ought rather to send to the ladies rose-coloured poems and baskets full of love-tales.

But no! I am still too near Paris. Every day, even among my pines, the capital splashes me with its melancholy. At the very hour that I write these lines, I learn of the wretched death of Charles Barbara, and my mill is mourning bitterly. Adieu, curlews and grasshoppers! I have now no heart for gayety. And that is why, madame, instead of the pretty, jesting story that I had determined to tell you, you will have again to-day a melancholy legend.

There was once a man who had a golden brain; yes, madame, a golden brain. When he came into the world, the doctors thought that the child would not live, his head was so heavy and his brain so immeasurably large. He did live, however, and grew in the sunlight like a fine olive-tree; but his great head always led him astray, and it was heartrend-ing to see him collide with all the furniture as he walked. Often he fell. One day he rolled from the top of a flight of stairs and struck his forehead against a marble step, upon which his skull rang like a bar of metal. They thought that he was dead; but on lifting him up, they found only a slight wound, with two or three drops of gold among his fair hair. Thus it was that his parents first learned that the child had a golden brain.

The thing was kept secret; the poor little fellow himself suspected nothing. From time to time he asked why they no longer allowed him to run about in front of the gate, with the children in the street.

"Because they would steal you, my lovely treasure!" his mother replied.

Thereupon the little fellow was terribly afraid of being stolen; he went back to his lonely play, without a word, and stumbled heavily from one room to another.

Not until he was eighteen years old did his parents disclose to him the miraculous gift that he owed to destiny; and as they had educated and supported him until then, they asked him, in return, for a little of his gold. The child did not hesitate; on the instant— how? by what means? the legend does not say—he tore from his brain a piece of solid gold as big as a nut, and proudly tossed it upon his mother's knees. Then, dazzled by the wealth that he bore in his head, mad with desires, drunken with his power, he left his father's house and went out into the world, lavishing his treasure.

From the pace at which he lived, like a prince, sowing gold without counting, one would have said that his brain was inexhausti- ble. It did become exhausted, however, and little by little one could see his eyes grow dull, his cheeks become more and more hollow. At last, one morning, after a wild debauch, the unfortunate fellow, alone among the rem- nants of the feast and the paling candles, was alarmed at the enormous hole he had already made in his ingot; it was high time to stop.

The Man with the Golden Brain

Thenceforth he led a new kind of life. The man with the golden brain went off to live apart, working with his hands, suspicious and timid as a miser, shunning temptations, trying to forget, himself, that fatal wealth which he was determined never to touch again. Unfortunately a friend followed him into the solitude and that friend knew his secret.

One night the poor man was awakened with a start by a pain in his head, a frightful pain. He sprang out of bed in deadly alarm, and saw by the moonlight his friend running away, with something hidden under his cloak.

Another piece of his brain stolen from him!

Some time after, the man with the golden brain fell in love, and then it was all over. He loved with his whole heart a little fair-haired woman, who loved him well, too, but who preferred her ribbons and her white feathers and the pretty little bronze tassels tapping the sides of her boots.

In the hands of that dainty creature, half

bird and half doll, the gold pieces melted merrily away. She had every sort of caprice; and he could never say no; indeed, for fear of causing her pain, he concealed from her to the end the sad secret of his fortune.

" We must be very rich," she would say.

And the poor man would answer:

" Oh, yes! very rich!" and he would smile fondly at the little bluebird that was innocently consuming his brain. Sometimes, however, fear seized him; and he longed again to be a miser; but then the little woman would come hopping towards him and say:

" Come, my husband, you are so rich, buy me something very costly."

And he would buy something very costly.

This state of affairs lasted two years; then, one morning, the little woman died, no one knew why, like a bird. The treasure was almost exhausted; with what remained the widower provided a grand funeral for his dear dead wife. Bells clanging, heavy coaches draped in black, plumed horses, silver tears on the velvet — nothing seemed too fine to him. What mattered his gold to him now? He gave of it for the church, for the bearers, for the women who sold immortelles; he gave it on all sides, without bargaining. So that, when he left the cemetery, almost nothing was left of that marvellous brain, save a few tiny pieces on the walls of his skull.

Then people saw him wandering through the streets, with a wild expression, his hands before him, stumbling like a drunken man. At night, at the hour when the shops were lighted, he halted in front of a large show-window in which a bewildering mass of stars and jewels glittered in the light, and he stood there a long while gazing at two blue satin boots bordered with swan's-down. "I know some one to whom those boots would give great pleasure," he said to himself with a smile; and, already forgetting that the little woman was dead, he went in to buy them.

From the depths of her back-shop, the dealer heard a loud outcry; she ran to the spot, and recoiled in terror at sight of a man leaning against the window and gazing at her sorrowfully with a dazed look. He held in one hand the blue boots trimmed with swan's-down, and held out to her the other hand all bleeding, with scrapings of gold on the ends of the nails.

Such, madame, is the legend of the man with the golden brain.

Although it has the aspect of a fanciful tale, it is true from beginning to end. There are, in this world many poor fellows who are contented to live on their brains, and who pay in refined gold, with their marrow and their substance, for the most trivial things of life. It is to them a pain recurring every day; and then, when they are weary of suffering——

The Three Low Masses

The Three Low Masses

A Christmas Tale

I

" TWO truffled turkeys, Garrigou ? "
" Yes, father, two magnificent turkeys stuffed with truffles. I know something
about it, for I myself helped to stuff them.
One would have said that the skin would
burst when they were roasting, it was distended so."

"Jesus-Maria! and I love turkeys so dearly,
Give me my surplice quickly, Garrigou. And
what else did you see in the kitchen besides
the turkeys ?"

" Oh, all sorts of good things. Since noon,
we have done nothing but pluck pheasants,
lapwings, pullets, chickens, and heath-cocks.
Feathers flew in every direction. And then

from the pond they brought eels, golden carp, trout, and——"

"How big are the trout, Garrigou?"

"As big as that, father. Enormous!"

"*Mon Dieu!* It seems to me that I see them. Did you put the wine in the cups?"

"Yes, father, I put the wine in the cups. But indeed! it is no such wine as you will drink before long, after the midnight mass. If you could just look into the dining-hall at the château, and see all those decanters, filled with wines of all colours. And the silver plate, the carved centrepieces, the flowers and the candelabra! Never again will such a *réveillon* [1] be seen. Monsieur the marquis has invited all the nobles of the neighbourhood. There will be at least forty at the table, without counting the notary and the bailiff. Ah! you are very fortunate to be one of them, father! Simply from smelling those fine turkeys, the odour of truffles follows me everywhere. Meuh!"

---

[1] *Réveillon,*—a late supper; a supper after midnight; specifically, a Christmas-eve feast or revel.—[Trans.]

The Three Low Masses

"Come, come, my boy! Let us beware of the sin of gluttony, especially on the eve of the Nativity. Go at once and light the candles, and ring the first bell for mass; for midnight is near at hand and we must not be late."

This conversation took place on Christmas night in the year of grace one thousand six hundred and something, between the Reverend Dom Balaguère, former prior of the Barnabites, and now stipendiary chaplain of the Lords of Trinquelage, and his little clerk Garrigou, or rather him whom he believed to be his little clerk Garrigou; for you must know that the devil on that evening had assumed the round face and insignificant features of the young sacristan, that he might the more easily lead the father into temptation and induce him to commit the frightful sin of gluttony. And so, while the pretended Garrigou (hum! hum!) made the bells of the seignorial chapel ring out lustily, the reverend father finished attiring himself in his chasuble, in the little sacristy of the château;

and, with his mind already perturbed by all these gastronomic details, he repeated to himself as he dressed:

"Roast turkeys, golden carp, and trout as big as that!"

Without, the night wind blew, scattering abroad the music of the bells, and one after another lights appeared in the darkness on the sides of Mount Ventoux, on the summit of which rose the ancient towers of Trinquelage. They were the families of the farmers, coming to listen to the midnight mass at the château. They climbed the hill singing, in groups of five or six, the father ahead, lantern in hand, the women enveloped in their ample dark cloaks, in which the children huddled together and sheltered themselves from the sharp air. Despite the hour and the cold, all those people walked cheerily along, upheld by the thought that, after the mass, there would be a table laid for them in the kitchens, as there was every year. From time to time, on the steep slope, the carriage of a nobleman, preceded by torch-bearers, passed with its windows gleaming in the moonlight like mirrors; or a mule trotted by, jingling his bells, and by the light of the mist-enveloped torches, the farmers recognised their bailiff and saluted him as he passed:

"Good evening, good evening, Master Arnoton!"

"Good evening, good evening, my children!"

The night was clear, the stars glistered more brightly in the frosty air; the wind had a sting in it, and a fine hoarfrost, which clung to the garments without wetting them, maintained faithfully the traditions of Christmas white with snow. At the summit of the hill, the château appeared as their destination, with its enormous mass of towers and gables, the steeple of its chapel rising into the blue-black sky; and a multitude of little twinkling lights, going and coming, flickering at every window, resembled, against the dark background of the building, sparks among the ashes of burnt paper.

The drawbridge and postern passed, they were obliged, in order to reach the chapel, to go through the first courtyard, filled with carriages, servants, bearers of sedan-chairs, brilliantly lighted by the flame of the torches and the blaze from the kitchens. One could hear the grinding of the spits, the clattering of the saucepans, the clink of the glasses and silverware, being moved about in preparation for the banquet, and over it all, a warm vapour, fragrant with the odour of roasting flesh and the pungent herbs of complicated sauces, led the farmers to say, with the chaplain and the bailiff and everybody else:

"What a fine *réveillon* we are going to have after mass!"

II

TING a ling! ting a ling, a ling!
That is the signal for the mass to begin. In the chapel of the château, a miniature

cathedral with intersecting arches and oaken wainscoting reaching to the ceiling, the tapestries have been hung and all the candles lighted. And such a multitude! and such toilets! First of all, seated in the carved pews which surround the choir, is the Sire de Trinquelage, in a salmon-coloured silk coat, and about him all the noble lords, his guests. Opposite, upon *prie-dieus* of silver, the old dowager marquise in her gown of flame-coloured brocade has taken her place, and the young Dame de Trinquelage, with a lofty tower of lace upon her head, fluted according to the latest style at the French court. Lower down, clad in black, with enormous pointed wings and shaven faces, are seen Thomas Arnoton the bailiff and Master Ambroy the notary, two sober notes among those shimmering silks and figured damasks. Then come the stout majordomos, the pages, the huntsmen, the stewards, and Dame Barbe with all her keys hanging at her side upon a slender silver ring. In the background, on the benches, sit the lesser functionaries, the maidservants and the farmers with their families; and lastly, at the farther end, against the door, which they open and close with care, the scullions come between two sauces to obtain a whiff of the mass, and to bring an odour of *réveillon* into the church, which is all in festal array and warm with the flame of so many candles.

Was it the sight of those little white caps which distracted the attention of the celebrant of the mass; was it not rather Garrigou's bell, that frantic little bell jingling at the foot of the altar with infernal precipitation, which seemed to be saying all the time:

"Let us hurry, let us hurry. The sooner we have finished, the sooner we shall be at the table."

The fact is that every time that that devil's own bell rang, the chaplain forgot the mass and thought only of the *réveillon*. He imagined the bustling cooks, the ovens beneath which a genuine forge fire was burning, the

steam ascending from the open saucepans,
and, bathed in that steam, two superb stuffed
turkeys, distended and mottled with truffles.

Or else he saw long lines of pages pass,
carrying dishes surrounded by tempting va-
pours, and entered with them the huge room
already prepared for the feast. O joy!
there was the enormous table all laden, and
blazing with light; the peacocks with all
their feathers, the pheasants flapping their
golden wings, the ruby-coloured decanters,
the pyramids of fruit resplendent amid the
green branches, and those marvellous fish
of which Garrigou had told him (ah, yes!
Garrigou indeed!) lying upon a bed of fennel,
their scales glittering as if they were fresh
from the water, with a bunch of fragrant herbs
in their monstrous nostrils. So vivid was the
vision of those marvels, that it seemed to Dom
Balaguère that all those wonderful dishes were
actually before him on the borders of the
altar-cloth; and two or three times, he surprised himself saying the *Benedicite,* instead

of the *Dominus vobiscum!* Aside from these slight mistakes, the worthy man read the service most conscientiously, without skipping a line, without omitting a genuflexion; and everything went well until the end of the first mass; for you know that on Christmas day the same celebrant must say three masses in succession.

"One!" said the chaplain to himself, with a sigh of relief; then, without wasting a minute, he motioned to his clerk, or to him whom he believed to be his clerk, and —

Ting a ling, a ling, a ling! ting a ling!

The second mass had begun, and with it began also Dom Balaguère's sin.

"Quick, quick, let us make haste!" cried Garrigou's bell in its shrill little voice; and that time the unhappy celebrant, wholly given over to the demon of gluttony, rushed through the service and devoured the pages with the avidity of his over-excited appetite. In frenzied haste he stooped and rose, made the signs of the cross and the genuflexions, and abridged all the motions, in order to have done the sooner. He barely put out his arms in the Gospel, he barely struck his breast at the *Confiteor*. The clerk and he vied with each other to see which could gabble faster. Verses and responses came rushing forth and tripped over one another. Words half pronounced, without opening the mouth, which would have taken too much time, ended in incomprehensible murmurs.

"*Oremus ps — ps — ps* ——"

"*Mea culpa — pa — pa* ——"

Like hurried vine-dressers, trampling the grapes into the vat, they both wallowed in the Latin of the mass, sending splashes in all directions.

"*Dom—scum!*" said Balaguère.

"*— Stutuo!*" replied Garrigou; and all the time the infernal little bell jangled in their ears like the bells that are put on post-horses to make them gallop at the top of their speed. As you may imagine, at that rate a low mass is soon despatched.

Alphonse Daudet

"Two !" said the chaplain, breathlessly; then, without taking time to breathe, flushed and perspiring, he ran down the steps of the altar, and——

Ting a ling, ling! ting a ling, ling!

The third mass had begun. He had but a few more steps to go to reach the banquet hall; but alas ! as the *réveillon* drew nearer, the ill-fated Balaguère was seized with a frenzy of impatience and gluttony. His vision became more vivid, the golden carp, the roast turkeys were there before him; he touched them; he—O Heaven! the dishes smoked, the wines scented the air; and the little bell, frantically shaking its clapper, shouted to him:

"Quicker, quicker, still quicker!"

But how could he go any quicker? His lips barely moved. He no longer pronounced the words. He could only cheat the good Lord altogether and filch the mass from Him. And that is what he did, the villain; passing from temptation to temptation, he began by skipping one verse, then two; then the Epistle was too long, and he did not finish it; he barely grazed the Gospel, passed the *Credo* without going in, jumped over the *Pater,* nodded to the Preface at a distance; and thus by leaps and bounds rushed into eternal damnation, still followed by the infamous Garrigou (get thee behind me, Satan !), who seconded him with wonderful alacrity, raised his chasuble, turned the leaves two by two, collided with the desks, overturned the communion-cups, and all the time shook the little bell louder and louder, faster and faster.

You should have seen the dismayed look on the faces of the whole congregation ! Obliged to follow by the pantomime of the priest the mass of which they did not hear a word, some rose while the others knelt, remained seated when the others were standing; and all the phases of that extraordinary service were confused upon the benches in a multitude of diversified attitudes. The Christmas star, travelling along the roads of the sky towards the little stable, turned pale with horror when it witnessed that confusion.

"The abbé goes too fast. No one can follow him," muttered the old dowager as she nodded her head-dress in bewilderment.

Master Arnoton, his great steel spectacles on his nose, looked through his prayer-book, trying to find out where they might be. But in reality, all those worthy folk, who also were thinking of the feast, were not sorry that the mass should travel at that lightning speed; and when Dom Balaguère, with radiant face, turned towards the congregation and shouted at the top of his voice: *"Ile, missa est,"* the whole chapel as with one voice responded with a *"Deo gratias"* so joyous, so infectious, that they fancied themselves already at table honouring the first toast of the *réveillon.*

<h2 style="text-align:center">III</h2>

FIVE minutes later the throng of nobles was seated in the great banquet-hall, the

chaplain among them. The château, illu-
minated from top to bottom, rang with songs
and shouts, and laughter and tumult; and the
venerable Dom Balaguère planted his fork in
the wing of a chicken, drowning his remorse
for his sin in floods of the Pope's wine and
in toothsome sauces. He ate and drank so
much, the poor holy man, that he died during the night of a terrible attack, without
even time to repent; then in the morning,
he arrived in heaven, which was still all
astir with the festivities of the night; and I
leave you to imagine how he was received
there.

"Depart from my sight, thou evil Christ-
ian!" said the Sovereign Judge, the Master of
us all. "Thy sin is monstrous enough to
efface a whole lifetime of virtue. Ah! thou
didst steal a mass from me. Even so! thou
shalt pay for three hundred masses in its
place, and thou shalt not enter paradise until
thou hast celebrated in thine own chapel
these three hundred Christmas masses, in the

presence of all those who have sinned with thee and by thy fault."

And this is the true legend of Dom Balaguère, as it is told in the land of olives. The château of Trinquelage does not exist to-day, but the chapel still stands erect on the summit of Mount Ventoux, in a clump of green oaks. The wind sways its disjointed door, the grass grows on the threshold; there are nests at the corner of the altar and in the embrasures of the tall windows, whence the stained glass long since vanished. But it appears that every year, at Christmas, a supernatural light wanders among the ruins, and that as they go to the midnight masses and the *réveillons,* the peasants see that spectral chapel lighted by invisible candles, which burn in the open air, even in the snow and the wind. You may laugh if you please, but a vine-dresser of the neighbourhood, named Garrigue, doubtless a descendant of Garrigou, tells me that one Christmas eve, being a little tipsy, he lost his way on the mountain towards Trinquelage; and this is what he saw. Until eleven o'clock, nothing. Everything was silent, dark, lifeless. Suddenly, about midnight, a carillon rang out at the top of the belfry; an old, old carillon, which seemed to be ten leagues away. Soon, on the road up the mountain, Garrigue saw flickering flames and vague shadows. Beneath the porch of the chapel, people walked and whispered:

"Good evening, Master Arnoton!"

"Good evening, good evening, my children."

When everybody had gone in, my vine-dresser, who was very courageous, noiselessly drew near, and looking through the broken door, saw a strange spectacle. All those people whom he had seen pass were arranged around the choir, in the ruined nave, as if the benches of olden time still existed. Fine ladies in brocade, nobles belaced from head to foot, peasants in gaudy jackets such as our great-grandfathers wore, and all with a venerable, faded, dusty, weary aspect. From time to time, night-birds, the ordinary occupants of the chapel, aroused by that blaze of light, fluttered about the candles, whose flames ascended straight towards heaven, as indistinct as if they were burning behind gauze; and one thing that amused Garrigue greatly was a certain individual with great steel spectacles, who kept shaking his old black wig, upon which one of those birds stood erect, with its feet entangled in the hair, silently flapping its wings.

In the background, a little old man, with a childish form, kneeling in the middle of the choir, shook desperately a tongueless, voiceless bell, while a priest, dressed in old gold, went to and fro before the altar, repeating prayers of which not a word could be heard. Beyond a doubt it was Dom Balaguère, saying his third low mass.

The Two Inns

The Two Inns

I WAS returning from Nîmes, one July afternoon. The heat was overwhelming. The
scorching white road stretched out as far as
the eye could see, a dusty line, between gar-
dens of olive-trees and of scrub-oaks, beneath
a huge sun of dull silver, which filled the whole
sky. Not a sign of shade, not a breath of
wind. Nothing save the vibration of the hot
air, and the shrill cry of the grasshoppers, a
mad, deafening music, at a hurried tempo,
which seemed the very resonance of that
boundless, luminous vibration. I had been
walking through this desert for two hours,
when suddenly a group of white houses de-
tached itself from the dust of the road before
me. It was what is called the relay of St.
Vincent: five or six farmhouses, long, red-
roofed barns, a watering-trough without
water, in a clump of meagre fig-trees, and, on

the outskirts of the hamlet, two large inns looking at each other from opposite sides of the street.

There was something striking in the proximity of those two inns. On one side, a large new building, full of life and animation, all the doors thrown open, the diligence stopping in front, the steaming horses being unharnessed, the passengers drinking hastily on the road, in the short shadow of the walls; the courtyard crowded with mules and vehicles; carters lying under the sheds, awaiting the cool of the evening. Within, outcries, oaths, blows of fists on the tables, the clinking of glasses, the clicking of billiard-balls, the popping of corks, and above all that uproar, a jovial, ringing voice, singing so loud that the windows shook:

> " Pretty little Margoton,
>   As soon as dawn was waking,
>   Took her silver pitcher,
>   And went off to the well."

The inn opposite, on the contrary, was

The Two Inns

silent and seemed deserted. Grass under the gateway, shutters broken, over the door a rusty twig of holly hanging like an old plume, the door-step strewn with stones from the road. It was all so poverty-stricken, so pitiful, that it seemed an act of charity to stop there and drink a glass.

On entering, I found a long room, deserted and dismal, which the dazzling light, entering through three curtainless windows, rendered even more dismal and deserted. A few rickety tables, on which stood broken glasses dull with dust, a dilapidated billiard-table, holding out its four pockets as if asking alms, a yellow couch, an old desk, slumbered there in an oppressive and unhealthy heat. And the flies! flies everywhere! I had never seen so many: on the ceiling, clinging to the windows, in the glasses, in swarms. When I opened the door, there was a buzzing, a humming of wings as if I were entering a hive.

At the end of the room, in a window-recess,

there was a woman standing close to the window, busily occupied in looking out. I called her twice:

"Ho there! hostess!"

She turned slowly, and showed me the face of a poverty-stricken peasant woman, wrinkled and furrowed, earth-coloured, framed by long lappets of rusty lace, such as the old women in our neighbourhood wear. She was not an old woman, though; but much weeping had faded her completely.

"What do you want?" she asked, wiping her eyes.

"To sit down a moment and drink something."

She gazed at me in amazement, without moving from her place, as if she did not understand me.

"Is n't this an inn?"

The woman sighed.

"Yes, it is an inn, if you choose. But why don't you go opposite, like all the rest? It is much more lively."

"It is too lively for me. I prefer to stay here with you."

And without waiting for her reply, I seated myself at the table.

When she was quite sure that I was speaking seriously, the hostess began to go and come with a very busy air, opening doors, moving bottles, wiping glasses, and disturbing the flies. It was clear that a guest to wait upon was an important event. At times the unhappy creature would stop and take her head in her hands, as if she despaired of ever accomplishing anything.

Then she went into the rear room; I heard her shaking great keys, fumbling with locks, looking into the bread-box, blowing, dusting, washing plates. From time to time a deep sigh, a sob ill stifled.

After a quarter of an hour of this business, I had before me a plate of raisins, an old loaf of Beaucaire bread, as hard as sandstone, and a bottle of sour new wine.

"You are served," said the strange creature;

and she turned back at once to her place at the window.

As I drank, I tried to make her talk.

"You don't often have people here, do you, my poor woman?"

"Oh, no! never any one, monsieur. When we were alone here, it was different; we had the relay, we provided hunt-dinners during the ducking-season, and carriages all the year round. But since our neighbours set up in business, we have lost everything. People prefer to go opposite. They consider it too dull here. It's a fact that the house is n't very pleasant. I am not good-looking, I have fever and ague, and my two little girls are dead. Over yonder, on the contrary, they are laughing all the time. It is a woman from Arles who keeps the inn, a handsome woman with laces, and three bands of gold beads round her neck. The driver of the diligence, who is her lover, takes it to her place. And then she has a lot of hussies for chamber-maids, so that she gets lots of custom! She has all the young men from Bezouces, Redessan, and Jonquières. The carters go out of their way to pass her house. And I stay here all day without a soul, eating my heart out."

She said this in a distraught, indifferent tone, with her forehead still resting against the glass. There was evidently something which interested her at the inn opposite.

Suddenly, on the other side of the road, there was a great commotion. The diligence moved off through the dust. I heard the cracking of the whip, the postillion's bugle, and the girls who had run to the door calling out:

"*Adiousias! adiousias!*" And over it all the stentorian voice that I had heard before, beginning again, louder than ever:

" She took her silver pitcher,
And went off to the well ;
From there she could not see
Three soldiers drawing near."

At that voice the hostess trembled in every limb, and, turning to me, she said in an undertone:

"Do you hear? That's my husband. Does n't he sing well?"

I gazed at her in stupefaction.

"What? Your husband? Do you mean to say that he goes there too?"

Thereupon, with a heart-broken air, but with the utmost gentleness, she replied:

"What can you expect, monsieur? Men are made that way; they don't like to see people cry; and I cry all the time since my little girls died. And then this great barrack, where nobody ever comes, is so melancholy. And so, when he is bored too much, my poor José goes across the road to drink, and as he has a fine voice, the woman from Arles makes him sing. Hush! there he goes again."

And she stood there, as if in a trance, trembling, with her hands outstretched, and tears rolling down her cheeks, which made her look uglier than ever, to hear her José singing for the woman from Arles:

"The first one said to her :
'Good day, my pretty dear !'"

Ingram Content Group UK Ltd.
Milton Keynes UK
UKHW021115180423
420361UK00006B/625

9 781360 188614